RUBBER SHARKS AND WOODEN ACTING

THE ULTIMATE BAD MOVIE GUIDE

This book can be
used to make
Tables less wobby.

Hurrah!,

RUBBER SHARKS AND WOODEN ACTING

THE ULTIMATE BAD MOVIE GUIDE

Nicko Vaughan

First published in the UK in 2016 by
Telos Publishing Ltd
5A Church Road, Shortlands, Bromley, Kent, BR2 0HP

www.telos.co.uk

Telos Publishing Ltd values feedback. Please e-mail us with any
comments you may have about this book to:
feedback@telos.co.uk

ISBN: 978-1-84583-940-6

Dedication

For my mum, Ruth, and my dad, Tony, who took me to the local video store every weekend and didn't complain when I kept renting the same film. You will be happy to know that *Misfits of Science* (1985) is still one of my favourite movies. For Nana, without whom I would have no sense of humour. For my other half Glenn, thanks for making me all of the tea when I was writing all of the words. For Cath, my BFF who complained only a tiny bit when I couldn't go out most Friday nights while I was writing this book. For Joe, my partner in crime, who started the Bad Film Club with me over ten years ago and who still craves bad movies and the word egg. And to everybody at the Bad Film Club who has put up with me showing them the most terrible films and has never physically attacked me. For Tony and for Chapter, who are still letting us play at their venue ten years on. But, most of all, thank you to the terrible filmmakers for keeping me off the streets.

Contents

Introduction

I've been wanting to write a book about my experiences with bad movies for a few years now, so when the charming people at Telos Publishing gave me the opportunity finally to write my thoughts down, I excitedly took them up on it. Then I spent my advance cheque. And then I started to panic a bit and continued to panic a lot for nine months. Have you ever tried to write a book? It's bloody hard work! They don't tell you that. You assume it's going to be all late nights in exclusive bars drinking absinthe and chatting to other authors about deadlines and difficult editors. I could swan about in coffee shops sipping lattes and tapping away at my laptop even though I don't drink coffee and my laptop is from 2002 with only a thirty minute battery life. But writing a book is not like that at all. For me, anyway, it was mostly sitting on my own at the computer wondering how many more words I should write before I allowed myself to have a biscuit and watch *Hell's Kitchen*.

But I've done it and, to be honest, I did rather enjoy it and I'm a little bit proud of it. As the gestation period was nine months I've named it 'my little book baby', and it shall remain the closest my parents are ever going to get to having grandchild. But, on the plus side, this book won't ever throw up over you on public transport or drain you of all your savings.

The internet has told me that part of my introduction should be about why I wrote the book and that I should also tell you all a bit about my background. As I imagine there exists some corny blurb on the back of this book that gives all the 'what', I shall speak a little bit of the 'how' and the 'why'.

Back in 2004 my comedy writing partner Joe Timmins and I were over in Melbourne doing the International Comedy

Festival. I don't know if you're aware of the sleep patterns of those attending a month-long comedy festival, but it goes a bit like this: 11.00 am, kind of wake up. 1.00 pm, actually wake up and then reluctantly get up for some food. 1.30 pm, eat some food and then mooch about the flat for a bit. 3.00 pm, vow to get up earlier the next day and enjoy more of the city. 5.00 pm, start thinking about getting dressed. 7.00 pm, leave the house for shows, drinks, socialising and performing. 1.00 am, go to some bar until you get kicked out. 4.00 am, bed. Repeat.

As you can see, there is a lot of dead time between shows when you do a festival. So Joe and I would spend that time watching a lot of movies on the television. It was the fourth day of the festival, and during a film called *Atomic Twister* (2002), that we discovered not only did we have a mutual love of bad movies, but we had a lot of fun showing them zero respect by talking all over them. We took this mutual love of bad films with us to the Edinburgh Fringe Festival in 2005 where, instead of lounging around in the flat waiting for the movies to come on the television, we left the flat and explored the many awesome second-hand DVD shops that Edinburgh has to offer. Three weeks and 75 DVDs later, there were more people in our flat watching us watching bad movies than there were at our actual Edinburgh show. So, one night, after lugging two guitars and a bag of props back to the flat, we started to talk about the idea of doing a show where we would improvise a commentary over bad movies. It would be doing something that we both enjoyed and that we could have enormous fun doing, and it also meant that we wouldn't have to lug a load of equipment from venue to venue.

To our astonishment, the lovely people at Chapter Arts Centre and the big old posh Barbican Centre in London took a chance on us, and on New Year's Day 2006 the Bad Film Club was born out of love, laziness and the unwillingness to get a proper job. Doing the Bad Film Club has given us an opportunity to talk to so many other lovers of bad movies and to indulge in a hobby that has shown us so many amazingly bad and strange celluloid wonders. Don't get me wrong, it's not all fun; some of the movies we've seen during the vetting processes have almost done us in. *Murder on Flight 502* (1975), *Species III* (2004) and *Inseminoid* (1981) all nearly killed us with boredom. But it's worth struggling through them, because the joy in finding a *good* bad movie makes the pain of watching dross easier to handle.

I think that one of the reasons I love bad movies so much is that they have an ability to morph into something new and entertaining; they make you see the film in a totally different way than was intended. It shows that film doesn't have to keep static, that even though a film may be unloved and outdated, somebody somewhere can still enjoy it. I also love how social bad movies can be. We are often told, especially in the UK, to be quiet in the cinema, to turn our phones off, to eat our snacks more quietly and to keep our fidgeting to a minimum. Bad movies allow us to talk as much as we want, to yell at the screen if we feel like it, to laugh with our friends; and if your phone goes off, you can take the call, it's not like you're going to be spoiling the movie for anybody else. It's strange that movies remain one of the last places where audiences can't interact with the product; television shows, radio shows and the internet have all found some way to involve the audience, be it playing games, voting for a variety act or taking part in a debate. Film, however, has been non-communicative since its invention. It's the media equivalent of an angry partner who has locked themselves in the bathroom during a fight. You can yell at that door all you like, you're only ever going to be met with silence. I believe that many people actually crave the ability to interact with their favourite movies, and this is why the *sing-a-long* series has become so popular. Interaction is also why hundreds of thousands of fans flock to late-night showings of *The Rocky Horror Picture Show* (1975) and *The Room* (2003); it's because they get to take part in the film, dress up and have conversations with the characters on the screen. If there was such a thing as a sing-a-long *Can't Stop the Music* (1980), I'd be there in a heartbeat. In fact, I'd probably be hosting it.

As a lover of bad movies, a film lecturer, and also somebody who has worked in the industry, I've tried to write with some insight into the mechanics of bad movies, giving you a blow-by-blow account of some of the classics as well as focusing on a few of the different genres. What I hope I've written is a book that is nestled somewhere between informative and autobiographical. There are also a couple of guides in here, one of which is how to safely watch a bad movie. If you're new to the dangers of watching terrible films, I suggest you skip to that chapter first; the advice and viewing guidelines it offers should be invaluable to prevent injury, both psychological and physical, if attempting to watch a bad movie for the first time. It also offers advice on other things such as how to plan your escape and what kind of snacks you might want to take with you.

If your favourite bad movie hasn't been mentioned in this book, I'm sorry. If I could have mentioned them all, I would have done, but I'm 42 now and I didn't relish the thought of still writing this book on my sixtieth birthday. I've tried to highlight the important plot points and flaws in a few of the 'classic' bad movies, and I would recommend those titles for anybody looking to have a fun bad movie with friends. I've also tried to stay away from the very early films, although *Reefer Madness* (1936) has managed to make it into the classic films section. You may notice that most of the films I talk about in this book are post-1975. This is the cut-off point we use for showing films as part of the Bad Film Club, and it is what we call the 'should know better by now' line in the sand. By this I mean that by 1975, filmmakers have learned a lot about how films are structured and how effects are created and used; the actors have grown up with sound, so can't use the 'I'm a silent film actor, I can't act with my voice' excuse, and camera technology is pretty decent. Audiences have seen *2001: A Space Odyssey* (1968), *Love Story* (1970) and *The Exorcist* (1970); they know how good films can be, so there shouldn't be any excuse *for C.H.O.M.P.S.* (1979), *Two of a Kind* (1983) or *Congo* (1995). Plus, going after *Forbidden Planet* (1956) or *Frankenstein Meets Wolf Man* (1943) would be like shooting fish in a barrel. Of course they are going to be rubbish; they were made in the same decades as kitty litter and the hula hoop were invented and when the charts were full of songs like 'ToolieOolieDoolie (The Yodel Polka)' by the Andrews Sisters. You can't expect a decade like that to succeed in producing a convincing science fiction movie; we were only just orbiting the Earth.

There will be a few film titles that you will undoubtedly see multiple times throughout this book: *Jaws The Revenge* (1987) and *Shark Attack 3* (2002) being two of my favourites. I love shark movies, and I love sharks. I make no apology for the probable shark bias within these pages. You would assume that a person who loves sharks so much would be averse to seeing them blown up, shot at and set on fire so many times. But no. I have seen every shark movie ever made, and that includes movies that aren't about sharks but just have the word shark in the title, like *Eagle vs. Shark* (2007).

I've also used our audience members at the Bad Film Club as a sounding board to try to answer the question, 'What makes a *good* bad movie?' Although bad-film lovers can be an eclectic bunch, I've offered a few key theories as to why some bad films turn *good* and some don't, as well as highlighting some of the common aspects found within nearly all of the bad-movie genres. And I do believe that bad movies are becoming a genre in their own right, just as the early B-movies of the 1960s broke free to become their own niche. Audiences have helped to create a modern day B-movie, but now the B doesn't represent the ranking status of a film that is supporting the main event, it stand for Bloody Awful, or Bollocks, or just plain Bad.

The bad-movie genre is most definitely split into two camps, the wilful and the accidental bad movie. It is an important distinction to make as, although both are classed as bad, their journey to that crappy destination is wildly different. In the accidental camp, audiences will find movies that haven't aged well, that focus around outdated political events or social ideologies or that were just really bad ideas in the first place. Here is where you will find movies such as *Commando* (1985), *Top Gun* (1986) and *Hackers* (1995). In *Hackers*, the technology alone is enough to send even the most novice computer user into a tailspin of ridicule. Lines like 'Zero Cool crashed 1,507 computers in one day. Biggest crash in history, front page *New York Times*' just sound cute now, especially in a time when 1,500 computers crashing wouldn't even make it to the daily company e-mail round-up let alone the front page of the *New York Times*. Watching *Hackers* in the 21st Century is like watching toddlers explaining how a washing machine works: creative and entertaining but, ultimately, nonsense.

The other camp is where you will find films made by studios that have gained momentum and publicity for their movies thanks to their high-profile internet viral marketing campaigns and ridiculously-titled bad movies. These studios are aware of the quality of their product and are setting out to make modern day schlock cinema. In the wilful camp is where you will find films from studios like The Asylum, whose titles include *Abraham Lincoln* vs. *Zombies* (2012) and the ever popular *Sharknado* (2013) series. It is also where you will find directors such as Roger Corman, who offers up titles like *Dinocroc*(2004) and *Attack of the 50ft Cheerleader* (2012). There can exist a little friction, sometimes, between fans of the two camps, with the wilfully bad movie fans being labelled fakers by the old school bad film fans, who argue that if a movie is aware that it is bad then it can't be a real bad movie. These companies can be likened to the makers of novelty soda flavours or ugly Christmas sweaters. Knowing that you are creating something bad on purpose is somehow cheating. But if *Sharknado* can tantalise a newbie over to the bad side and into films like *Disco Godfather* (1979) or *Aerobicide* (1987), then surely that's a good thing.

Put simply, regardless of the intentions of the production companies, the actors or the distributors, I love any and all bad movies, and I am always looking to share rare finds, new low-budget stinkers and lowlights from the classic bad movies with other people who are as enthusiastic as I am. This book is intended to be a light-hearted journey of my misadventures with bad movies, and I hope you enjoying reading it, mostly because it took me bloody ages to write. Again, they just don't tell you how much time you have to spend on these things. It should be the first thing on the contract: 'By the way, you are going to yell at your boyfriend/girlfriend a lot while doing this.' If nothing else, it affords me one extra gift to give to my parents at Christmas. I hope you enjoy it.

1
In Search of the *Good* Bad Movie

To the majority of people, actually paying money to sit through a terrible movie is not only an alien concept but also a ridiculous one. Why, after working hard all week, would anybody choose to spend their hard-earned cash watching shoddily-put-together plots performed by actors whose only skill is to eyebrow act their way through a scene? But to me, and a growing number of others like me, the idea is not only normal, it's irresistibly seductive.

What has been the most enjoyable thing about running the Bad Film Club for ten years is having the opportunity to sit in a room with like-minded people who get just as excited about watching terrible movies on the big screen, or more realistically medium screen, as I do. Like most bad-movie lovers, my 'normal' circle of friends have no interest in these kinds of movies and would turn their noses up at the chance to see *Troll 2* (1990) or *Megaforce* (1982). In fact, a lot of them judge my choices and question if I am in my right mind, even going so far as to mock the films I love. They don't understand that going to see *Captain America* (2014) at the cinema is as 'enjoyable' for me as it is for them to go out and 'enjoy' *All About Steve* (2009). Just because more people saw *Captain America* doesn't mean that it's a more valid cinematic choice. (Don't even get me started on Captain America. He really is the dullest of all the superheroes; dry-cleaning Superman's underpants would be more interesting to watch than that sanctimonious walking flag pin.) To be in a room with 400 other bad film aficionados all cheering at the awful special effects in *Speed 2* (1997), or clutching spoons and tossing around American footballs before a showing of *The Room* (2003), is a wonderful thing to experience. These people don't judge you because of your film choices, they love you for them, and they will talk to you about their favourite bad movies and give you more suggestions of even worse movies you can try. They are the pimps of bad cinema, starting you off with a soft, mildly offensive bad movie like *Sex and the City* (2008) and then slowly increasing the strength until you are mainlining the hard stuff like Uwe Boll's *House of the Dead* (2003). I hold my hands up: I am one of those pimps, an evangelist for cinematic crap and a spokesperson for the straight-to-DVD community.

In the past, bad movies were seen as a guilty pleasure, a secret pastime that only a few people indulged in, but now the practice is growing in popularity. This could be, in some way, thanks to broadcasters like the SyFy Channel and online production hoovers such as Netflix needing to buy in as much cheap product as possible to bolster their content. There is also now an abundance of movie channels that live a long way south from where the prime packages live, and they also need low-budget movies to fill up their airtime. This popularity has led to an increase in companies finding and distributing bad movies, as more and more people are seeking them out.

The idea of watching a bad movie on purpose may still be an alien one to many people, but it is spreading fast, much like a military mutated deadly virus, as increasing numbers jump on the bandwagon to enjoy what terrible movies have to offer.

One of the most frequent questions I get asked is, 'What makes a *good* bad movie?' And that is a really difficult question to answer, because although we can be pretty sure what will make an audience cry or even laugh, it's hard to pinpoint a type of bad movie that will be enjoyed by the majority and that doesn't make people want to staple their eyes shut as the end credits roll. I can try to explain the *good* bad movie phenomenon only from my own personal experiences. I've calculated that I've spent four years of my life, so far, watching terrible movies. I could have spent that time getting a medical degree instead of buggering about watching CGI sharks, but luckily for me, I can't stand the sight of blood. In that time, I've seen exceptional displays of bad acting, unfeasible plot lines and dreadful executions of the simplest concepts come together within a 90-minute time-frame. When it is done 'right', the resulting magical cocktail produces a film that somehow transforms the original product into its opposite and creates something beautiful; our own bad-film Goldilocks zone if you like.

A *good* bad film also has the ability to switch genres. Take, for example, an action crime thriller like *Firestorm* (1998); it's a film about a forest fireman's attempts to bring to justice the most evil mock-Canadian murdering prison escapee while, at the same time, fleeing a raging forest fire with a CIA-trained ornithologist who has been kidnapped. The outlandishly stupid nature of the plot and painful acting turn the film from an action thriller into a slapstick comedy. But this is an unintentional comedy, one where you are laughing at them, not with them. For example, the gang leader of the escaped cons, Shaye, played by William Forsyth, keeps murdering members of his gang of criminals without anybody becoming suspicious. It's laughable, and that absurdity gains momentum as the film ticks along, due to the fact it keeps happening and still nobody notices.

'Hey, where did Roy go?'

'He fell off the cliff.'

'I swear that Steve was here a moment ago.'

'He accidentally set himself on fire and burned alive in the cabin.'

'Did anybody notice were Dave went?'

'An eagle swooped down and took him away.'

I am convinced that a *good* bad movie has the ability to tap into something deep within a person's brain and play about with the part that creates joy when faced with misfortune. The question that should be addressed, even if there is no definitive answer, is: how can anybody enjoy something so terrible and not only be entertained but keep going back for more? It is more than a kind of *schadenfreude*, because instead of taking pleasure in the misfortune of others, the viewer is enjoying the misfortune they are putting themselves through. Perhaps a new phrase should be coined, something like *schadenfreude-masochism*, the enjoyment of the lasting pain a bad movie causes to your soul. The sense of achievement in finding a film that has the alchemy within it to create something new, should also not be overlooked. Finding a rare gem of a bad movie ignites our reward system and showers us in dopamine until we crave more of it.

The enjoyment could be perceived in the same context as that gained by a housewife or a student watching programmes like *The Jeremy Kyle Show*. The pleasure of watching these modern-day freak shows is derived not only from the misery of others, but also from the relief of knowing that it's not you on stage wearing jeggings and getting yelled at because of your social standing. In a similar way, watching bad movies could make the viewer feel superior, more talented and with the intelligence to understand that you shouldn't shoot a close-up of a person wearing mirrored sunglasses. It doesn't matter what the angle is, Roy, we're always going to be able to see the crew. The problem I have with that theory is that I don't consider myself to be superior to these films. In fact I am sometimes humbled by their blatant and uncloseted badness. It's more admiration than mockery. Give me a time machine and the opportunity to work either with Martin Scorsese as he's directing *Goodfellas* (1990) or David Worth as he's directing *Shark Attack 3* (2002) and I'd be right there with my wetsuit on and a tin of polystyrene shark primer at the ready. Yes, we are laughing at your work because your work is ridiculous, but we love you for it and we live in hope that you will make more of it.

In a conversation I had about bad movies with comedian and writer Cody Whitaker, he described a good bad film as being like 'a charismatic failed experiment', and said that although a bad movie is made with good intentions, it ends up being unrealistic and poorly-made simply because a competent level of skill and creativity is not present in the filmmakers.

These charismatic failures seduce audiences into coming back to them time and time again. Cody went on to talk about his relationship with bad movies and, in particular, one of his favourite *good* bad movies, *Baby Boy* (2001), a film he describes as 'incredibly facile and stupid'. Even though the film scores a high 69% rating on Rotten Tomatoes and is generally well reviewed by critics, Cody obviously doesn't agree with the positive ratings, because to him it's a bad movie: 'While watching [the movie], I was constantly thinking, *God this dialogue is stupid and condescending*, but all the while I found it funny for the same reason.' Even though he finds the movie frustrating, something keeps pulling him back to watch it multiple times. Again, it's that *schadenfreude*-masochism taking hold and creating an addiction.

Another Bad Film Club audience member I spoke to about the reasons why some people choose to watch bad movies was Edmund Schluessel, a part-time bad-movie connoisseur and full-time theoretical astrophysicist. Edmund pointed out, 'A *good* bad movie helps highlight what we like about good movies.' His favourite bad movie of choice is the classic *Manos: The Hands of Fate* (1966). This is well known to those in the bad film community for being an unimaginative and ordinary movie that gets almost every element of filmmaking wrong. Edmund said of the film: 'Everything is so badly done that it makes immersing yourself in the world of the film and suspending disbelief impossible. Every shot is out of focus, the incidental music is distracting and the voices are dubbed and out of sync.' By Edmund's logic, the fact that the film is so monumentally flawed makes the viewer hyper-aware of the artistry and skill needed to make a good movie; and so, during a bad movie, you could be retroactively appreciating movies you've taken for granted in the past. You're creating another level of enjoyment. He also went on to say that watching bad movies could actually put the viewer into 'a state of critical self-awareness and deconstruction where we are reminded of how, in a good film, the camerawork highlights important elements and how good incidental music reinforces or even sets a scene'.

This is a perceptive point as, in my experience, the people who are lovers of really bad movies are the same people who are fans of high art and good-quality cinema as well.

There is a difference between a *good* bad movie and a *bad* bad movie, and those who have more than just a functioning interest in cinema are able to tell them apart. What neither side are interested in is the cinema that is *in between*. The dull cinema, the movies that can't even raise an eyebrow of interest, the ones that are not quite good enough to be watchable and not quite bad enough to be entertaining. These movies meander around in the grey areas, boring us with their middle-of-the-road acting and predictably dreary generic narratives. Not even a bad-film lover relishes watching them. They are an ordeal to sit through; each minute feels like ten as you try to convince yourself that surely it has to land on one or the other side of the film spectrum. Instead it flails in the middle, lethargic and unyielding, leaving you unsatisfied and feeling as though you've aged ten years.

My Bad Film Club partner, Joe, recalls some of the movies that have tested even our high tolerance since we started watching bad movies together over ten years ago. He notes that *Murder on Flight 502* (1975) was a particularly difficult one: 'It's your typical 1970s airline disaster movie that stretched what was, at best, a half hour *Colombo* episode into an hour and forty minutes of misery. Real misery. Abject, lime-in-the-eye bloody misery. I remember we had to watch it in stages.' The stages Joe mentions were actually half-hour sections in which we watched the film between cups of tea, bottles of beer and other movies. The film was so slowly paced that at one point we both fell asleep and then had to rewind it, because that is how determined we were to get to finish it. And finish it we did; but it is not something I would want to sit through again.

What helped cement my understanding of the elements that help create a *good* bad movie was being asked to take part in Mark Watson's 27-hour show in aid of Comic Relief. Our contribution was to watch 27 hours of bad movies in one sitting, which sounded easy. After all, we watch bad movies all the time; what's the difference in watching them all in one go? I'll tell you what the difference is: it's the hallucinating that you're in a restaurant, the talking to an empty chair and the feeling as though you want to jump out of a window just to escape the badness for a little while. Despite the odd mental crack, we managed to complete the task and watched a total of 15 films in a row. The interesting thing about watching that many films back-to-back is that, regardless of genre, you get to notice the recurring themes, patterns and techniques that worm their way into almost all of the *good* bad movies we enjoy. So, as well as the movie having the ability to become the opposite of its intention and the ability to swap genres, a *good* bad movie should also include the following:

The abuse of stock footage

The advent of HD has not been kind to the makers of bad movies, because the relatively poor image quality of pre-2005 stock footage included in a film makes it stick out a mile. Either the filmmakers don't care or they edit their films on really tiny screens where the marked difference between specially-filmed action and stock footage goes unnoticed. On a good quality television or on a medium-sized cinema screen, however, the transition from smooth and focused camerawork to grainy, almost Pathéstyle footage reveals itself as being as obviously fake as Gerard Butler's American accent in every film he's ever made. The biggest abuse of stock footage comes from my beloved *Shark Attack 3* (2002), where it intrudes into the action so much it almost becomes a character. There are so many instances of stock footage abuse in this film that it feels as though they shot only about 40 minutes of original material. There is the hilarious overuse of 'bitey shark coming out of the water' footage, which the filmmakers have superimposed and made comically giant in order to represent the prehistoric megalodon shark roaming the waters just off the coast of Mexico. To add to the absurdity, the producers have also demonstrated a flagrant disregard for any logical sense of scale, as the shark keeps changing size depending on what it's chomping on. At one point it eats a speedboat and then a jet ski, both of which manage to fit snugly into the inside of its gob, despite the differences in size. But this is not the best abuse of stock footage *Shark Attack 3* has to offer. It's not even the addition of shark footage with a tiny CGI yellow submarine containing John Barrowman that takes the prize. There is one scene earlier in the film where the footage combines the double whammy of not only being of very poor quality but also of being surplus to the plot. If we were to examine the film more closely we might find that most of the scenes are actually surplus to the plot; there are times when the plot is even surplus to the plot; but you get my meaning.

This particular scene takes place on a boat where a middle-aged fisherman is struggling with something on the end of his line as, right behind him, a scantily-clad young woman and sketchy-looking man engage clumsily and feverishly in pre-sex-having. It's never made clear if the fisherman is the young woman's father, but if he is, he certainly has very fast and loose ideas about parenting. If that was me, I'm confident that my father would, at the very least, politely ask me to take my sex-having out of his peripheral vision. It's not just the inappropriate nature of the scene or the juddering and gyrating of the couple that makes the whole thing baffling, it's the splicing in of what appears to be 1960s-shot footage of swordfish. In fact it looks so bad and out of place that I would happily accept a sock puppet or even a drawing of a swordfish as a more plausible representation. Back and forth within the scene the footage merrily pops. We go from old man struggling to catch a fish, to pre-sex-having, to more struggling, to more footage, back to the fisherman, then back to the pre-sex-having and so on, until the head of the swordfish is reeled in. The contrast of the grainy, out-of-focus footage cutting to the bright digital clarity of the specially-shot material and then back again is like a slow strobe light, and serves only to highlight the absurd pointlessness of the scene and the 'meh' attitude of the filmmakers. Validity of the scene aside, somebody should have had the decency to tell the fisherman that, judging by the quality and age of the stock footage, the fish he was trying to catch was at least fifty years in the past. He had no chance. I understand that using stock footage is much cheaper than going out to film new material, and that resorting to the use of CGI on a budget can lower the quality of your film. But when your stock footage is so bad it makes audiences wonder if they've accidentally stepped back in time, it might be worth a rethink.

The use of science

No bad movies bring me more joy than those that harness the power of science. I'm not talking about science fiction movies or those that focus on science and discovery, I'm talking about those that sporadically use 'science' as a means to provide an easy plot resolution, or to try to explain the existence of a giant killer rabbit or why a person has suddenly turned into a tree. And in *good* bad movies, the indication to the audience that science is being used is that it can be seen bubbling away in tubes and beakers in stark rooms with minimal lighting.

Science is represented in all its forms within the bad movie family. In the Nu Image classic *Hammerhead* (2005) – also known as *SharkMan* – it is used to try to create a shark-human hybrid as a possible cure for cancer. Unfortunately science can't stop the shark babies from biting their way out of their human mothers' wombs, and 'death by tiny shark vagina trauma' is almost impossible to put down, unquestioned, on a death certificate. In *The Mutations* (1974) – also known as *The Freakmaker* – the bubbling science is used to try to genetically combine people with plants to create walking bushes. Here the science is not only bubbling but is also used to demonstrate interesting breakthroughs. We see a twig that bleeds when cut with a scalpel, a live rabbit being fed to a hungry plant that greedily gobbles it up, and humans who turn into killer bushes and die. 'Death by murderous shrubbery transmutation' is also difficult to put down, unquestioned, on a death certificate. In both

Hammerhead and *The Mutations,* science is used to experiment on humans, because science is evil and it will not rest until we are all part shark or part shrub. One of the my favourite uses of the 'science montage' can be found in Jack Perez's film *Mega Shark vs. Giant Octopus* (2009), another Asylum-produced winner, which tells the horrific tale of a prehistoric shark and octopus that are accidentally released from their icy holding pen. Now free and still a bit cross, they battle it out, trying to kill each other and destroy bits of America in the process. In this dangerous world, 1980s pop singer Debbie Gibson is an oceanographer and rebel who enjoys taking expensive experimental equipment out for a joyride. A little while into the film, all of the scientists try to find a solution to the large and troublesome shark and octopus 'fighting each other while destroying landmarks' problem. Some time after a rather awkward sex-having scene in a cupboard amongst a lot of mops and bleach (because nothing makes people horny like trying to destroy prehistoric sea giants ... am I right, fellas?), Gibson's character realises that she can solve the problem of the huge grumpy shark and grumbly octopus by using sex science. (Shut up: yes, it is a thing.) All they need is a chemical to mimic the scents given off by the creatures when they are feeling a little amorous. The creatures will be attracted to the scent, find each other, and then, *boom!*, fight to the death and stop taking it out on America, its landmarks and its innocent aeroplanes. And what better cue for a 'science montage' is there then a team of boffins looking for a chemical sex-having hormone?

During the montage there are a lot of rejected science results, as each actor takes the opportunity to brush up on his best 'science acting' by looking down a microscope, shaking his head. Obviously this science is far too small. Next they try pouring red science from one beaker into another while shoving some purple science into a tube that is almost brimming over with other purple science. Nothing. The double purple science is a dead end; how could they have even thought that similar-coloured science was going to work? Next they try pouring some blue science from a tube into a small amount of red science. *Damn it!* The frustration is clearly written all over their faces; or it would be if they were better actors. More depictions of small bottles containing a rainbow of liquids next to giant tubes of science are met time and time again with the disappointed faces of scientists running out of different coloured science to use. Even a pipette of light blue science dropped into a vat of yellow science does nothing. And then, just when it seems that all hope is lost, they crouch behind a table, as is the traditional science stance, and pour *clear* science into yellow science. It works. We know it works, because it starts to glow in the dark. It would seem that the science they were looking for was the same science that toy manufacturers used to make tiny glow-in-the-dark stars that you stick to your ceiling to make it come alive at night. Hurray for glowing science saving the day.

At least *Mega Shark vs. Giant Octopus* is using science for good. In most *good* bad movies it is used for evil, and mostly military evil. I would have thought scientists had enough to deal with, trying to save the world from diseases and new biological threats, without having to fanny about creating a chair that knows kung fu. Does the world really need a genetically-mutated giant spider to help fight the war on terror? Do we need sharks that can solve a Rubik's cube? Human hybrids? Killer rats? Don't we have nuclear weapons, and aren't they more effective than a duck with a laser beak? Maybe the military need to stop dicking about with these things and understand that a bomb and a gun are more effective than a human with a dorsal fin. It never, *ever* ends well for them.

Use of technology and the internet

Second only to my love of bad movie science is my love of bad movie technology. As technology evolves at such a great speed, it's baffling to think why a filmmaker would include it in a movie when it will only make the movie look laughably dated in a few years' time. In addition, it is clear that a lot of bad-film makers don't really understand how the technology works in the first place. The result is having technology behave in a way that is highly unrealistic and ludicrous. I often wonder if the reason why technology evolves and develops at such a staggering rate is that computer bods have to keep up with the unrealistic big-screen depictions of its abilities, which audiences then come to expect from the real world. I'm going to use my beloved *Shark Attack 3* as an example again.

There is a wonderful scene where John Barrowman's lifeguard character is curious to find out more about the shark tooth he has pulled from some underwater fibre-optic cables while diving for dinner during his beach patrol. He does what everybody does when needing answers: he gets out his laptop and searches the internet. But this is no ordinary laptop. First he's on what looks like an official marine biology department's website, a lovely white page with a massive header that screams 'MARINE TECH', and here he searches for 'shark teeth'. After a page of pictures of various shark teeth is returned, he scrolls down each one, playing the little known game of 'digital shark tooth snap'. To play the game, you simply hold an object next to a screen of pictures of other objects similar to yours in the hope that you find a match. It also helps if the computer can make a strange beeping sound every time it scrolls, so that the viewer really gets a sense that something is happening, when clearly it isn't. Sadly there are no matches, so he decides to tell the world about his discovery – well, to post it on the Marine Tech website. But he needs a picture. Luckily, next to his computer is a digital camera. It's one of those magic cameras from the future; you know, the ones where even though it's not plugged into anything it can take a picture of an object, correct the angle it was shot at, remove the hand that is holding it, eliminate all of the background and instantly send it to the laptop. Such a clever device. If you would like to buy one of these cameras you can order them at the Have 2035 Technology Today online store. After the picture is posted under the heading 'Mystery Shark', the page is then viewed by another interested party, but her computer has changed it to 'Mistery Shark'; and after careful thought I have concluded that Miss Tery Shark must have been her real name. Nobody during the making of that scene cared about the logic of technology, they just cared about getting to the scenes with the big shark. It's what I have named the 'Oh, balls to it, Steve, that will do' method of filmmaking.

Turbulence 3 (2001) suffers even more from the effects of dated technology and clueless filmmakers. This movie manages to bring to the surface nearly every cliché involving modern technology, including the often used but never understood line, 'You hacked into the mainframe.' In bad movies, hackers are always hacking into the mainframe. They love mainframes. Even though companies rarely use mainframes, and even if they did, hacking into one isn't going to shower the 'hacker' with an untold bounty of informational treasure, it's more likely to show him Dave from accounting's high score in solitaire. The subplot of *Turbulence 3* is that a rock concert happening on an aeroplane is being shown online, and this is such a big deal that the internet has been borrowed and is being contained in a large room for the evening. It even has a dedicated wall-mounted screen counting, on what looks like a website made of stone, the 'hits' that the stream is attracting. This constantly-changing series of numbers ticks up from 1,979,000 near the start to a whopping 3,006,333, which almost breaks the internet. Imagine a world where an online video can attract just over three million people! Meanwhile, over on YouTube, a kitten having a bath with a foam duck just reached 120 million.

The whole technology set-up is idiotic, and the 'hacker' doesn't do anything to dissuade from that opinion. He's hacking into the system with his bundle of computers and his floppy discs to piggyback the stream and watch it for free. If he would just wait a day he could probably download it from a torrent site. It also appears to be rather easy to hack any and all systems with just a flick of the keyboard. It's always so easy to hack into anywhere when you are in a bad film. Some super-bad guy or maverick detective might order an on-screen nerd (you know them: comic book T-shirt, greasy hair and awkward demeanour) to hack into a seemingly non-hackable system. 'I need you to break into Pentagon's computer.' To which the reply is almost always, 'There's no way I can hack into that, it's the goddamn Pentagon,' and then after a few taps of the keyboard, 'Okay, I'm in.' I often wonder how they access it so easily when it can take me hours to create a new password for my Gmail account. Maybe hacking is a lot simpler than we think it is. Perhaps it's just a case of putting 'super-secret Pentagon password' into Google and taking it from there. Note: I just Googled 'super-secret pentagon password', and apparently it's 'Swordfish'. Maybe it really is that easy.

Background music and sound effects

I get it, music is expensive. It's one of the reasons why, when the British television channel Dave repeats *Top Gear*, they replace *The A Team* theme tune with a Nokia 3310 ringtone. But has anybody thought that, maybe, no music is better than bad music? Nothing signposts a shitty movie more than badly-made and intrusive background music that seemingly never ends. Worse than loud and obnoxious music is background music that is completely inappropriate to the action. In the film *Dungeons and Dragons* (2000), there are instances of rapturous music, swelling strings and heroic brass, even when the main character is just wandering around eating an apple. In *Firestorm* (1998), the soft cock-rock music coupled with the slow-motion rescue scenes makes the entire film feel like a shampoo commercial. Take two bottles into the shower? Not me, my hair was burned off by a falling tree that was on fire.

The most annoying and noticeable background music intrusion comes from the most un-festive Christmas movie, *Santa's Summerhouse* (2012), where nearly every scene is filled with the kind of Christmas carol tunes you find in those annoying cards that play music when you open them. Tinny, brash-sounding renditions of seasonal songs seemingly blasted from the speakers of a 1980s Casio keyboard are liberally dowsed over every single piece of the action; be it comedic or dramatic, it makes no difference, the noise is constant. It's never more noticeable than in the 12-and-a-half-minute croquet scene, something I will tell you more about in the chapter on Christmas movies. For 12-and-a-half minutes of very little dialogue, the music consists of one loud and long honking, crappy mess after another, to the point where I started to forget what the concept of silence was. 'Jingle Bells' played on a kazoo and 'We Wish You a Merry Christmas' deafeningly parped out of a toy trumpet are enough to make you yearn for Cliff Richard. But not in a sexual way; or, if in a sexual way, it's your twisted fantasy.

As I said earlier, I understand that music is expensive, and so low-budget movies are going to struggle. However, sound effects shouldn't be that difficult to create. Most people are aware that when studios shoot a movie they are aiming for something called clean sound; that is, the only sound that can be heard during the playback is the actors' voices. All other sounds are added by amazing foley artists who replicate everything from decapitation to a cold can of soft drink being placed on a glass coffee table. I've always wanted to be a foley artist. I spent an hour once trying to create the perfect 'throwing up in a bucket' sound effect for a radio piece we were recording. It was so much fun. In case you're wondering, the best sound comes from a washing up bowl with an inch of water having a container of loose porridge mixed with a can of mushrooms sploshed into it from a great height. A good foley artist's work will be undetectable and realistic and should in no way distract the audience from the action. The bad foley artist's work will have audiences struggling to hear the actors speak over the noise their jumpers are making. Classic examples here range from *Snow Beast* (1977), which features the world's heaviest boots, loudest snow and noisiest doors, to *Jaws The Revenge* (1987), where the killer shark manages to roar like a lion even though sharks have no organs for producing sound.

Take all of the above elements, combine them with bad acting, bad narrative and genre-changing properties, and you have yourself a perfect storm. These are the main qualities that a film must encompass in order to attain that mythical *good* bad movie status.

2

The Classics: A Blow by Blow of Films that Blow

Apart from being asked what makes a bad movie, the other questions I most frequently get asked are which bad film is my favourite, and which bad films would I recommend?

Recommending a *good* bad movie can be difficult, because bad-film fans, much like parents (if they're honest), all have their favourites. My collection is overflowing with shark movies, from the classic *Jaws* (1975)and *Deep Blue Sea* (1999) to the lesser-known *Spring Break Shark Attack* (2005) and *Jaws 5: Cruel Jaws* (1995). What do you mean, you never knew they made a *Jaws 5*? It's a cinematic classic from filmmaker Bruno Mattei, featuring some skilful footage butchery from *Jaws, Deep Blood* (1990) and *The Last Shark* (1981). Basically it's the same old story of a shark terrorising a town, but this one features a Hulk Hogan lookalike and a little girl who is crippled, but only on land. Seek it out, it's epically bad.

A person's predilection for bad movies is as unique as a snowflake. Some are drawn to big 1980s action movies; some love the guts and gore of 1960s slasher horror movies; a handful prefer the gentle soft focus of biopic films usually found on the Hallmark channel; and there are those who can't get enough of low-budget creature-features. We all of us have our 'brands', and so matching the film to the person can be tricky. Recommend the wrong film to the wrong person and you could easily be branded a charlatan. But even though most fans of terrible cinema might state a preference, there are certain classic bad movie titles that most would agree are almost universally enjoyable. Some may even call them classic bad movies. Despite the fact that they don't conform to their chosen genre, most can agree there are some that are well worth watching, whatever you're into.

To help and encourage those bad-movie novices who are looking to dip their toe into the cinematic world of the *good* bad movie, I have outlined below a few of the titles most requested and recommended by bad-film fans at late-night movie-house showings up and down the country. I've outlined their plotlines and a few of the best scenes in the hope that this will give you a feel for the film, so that if you do take the plunge and watch any of them, there won't be any nasty surprises. I am hesitant to call these 'spoilers', because giving a spoiler alert kind of implies that what you are about to say might spoil a person's enjoyment of a film. In this case, the films are already spoiled, so it doesn't make much of a difference. Think of the following as more like a pamphlet of health and safety information. Forewarned is forearmed, and all that. Rubber gloves on and protective breathing apparatus at the ready, let's delve into some *good* bad movie recommendations.

Jaws The Revenge

Number four of the official *Jaws* movies and one of my all-time favourite films is *Jaws The Revenge* (1987). You've got to feel sorry for the Brody family: their lives are perpetually interrupted by a series of angry giant sharks. You'd think it would be enough to make them all move inland to somewhere like Utah or Arizona and get a job in a call centre, but they never learn. In *Jaws The Revenge*, Sean Brody (Mitchell Anderson) still lives with his mum on Amity Island and works as a police deputy, following in the footsteps of his father. Chief Brody is unfortunately now deceased because, as Ellen Brody (Lorraine Gary) puts it, he was thinking about sharks all of the time and had a heart attack. Sean's brother Michael (Lance Guest) lives away and is a marine biologist who tracks sea snails for a university. Yes, you can do that as an actual job.

The film opens just before Christmas, with Sean being sent out to free a log that has become trapped on a buoy and is posing a threat to shipping in the area. The fact that the log is on a buoy that is specifically designed to tell ships to steer clear of an area due to hazards, even going so far as to have a flashing light on the top, is never mentioned. So, out pops Sean, scampering into his boat, in the dead of night, to clear the hazard warning buoy of a hazard that the hazard buoy is specifically designed to warn against. Did I mention it is just before Christmas? Off he goes to poke a small log and a buoy with a stick that looks like its not quite long enough. There is no impending doom here; it's nearly Christmas, there's a small log on a buoy just out of reach, nothing to see, move along. Just a short stick and a well-meaning man. However, as Sean reaches over to try to free the troublesome log while wearing an overly baggy waterproof jacket (and there is nothing unusual about wearing an oversized jacket, a jacket so big that you could hide an arm inside it if you needed to; nope, nothing unusual in that at all), suddenly out of nowhere appears the snarling pointy end of a giant shark. *Growl! Snarl!* Poor Sean staggers back with no arm. No, that is not an arm-shaped lump under his oversized waterproof jacket; the shark has just taken his arm and managed to leave behind a lot of the jacket sleeve. With no arm, and soon no anything else, Sean is quickly devoured by the shark. But this is no ordinary shark. Not only has it managed to work out Sean's shift patterns, it's made sure the other cop on duty is busy with cow tippers and has managed to wedge a log into a buoy, despite having no arms. It also proves clever enough to sink the boat to hide the evidence. Of course, the real tragedy of this scene is that the log on the buoy is never moved and so continues to pose a threat to shipping.

After Sean's funeral, his brother Michael, who has the longest legs in film history and the most annoying daughter, decides that it's in his mother's best interests to leave the coastal town of Amity Island. The water is a constant reminder of the harrowing deaths of her son and her husband, and so she should move in with him, his wife and their annoying child at their oceanfront house in the Bahamas. As Michael points out to his mother, it's not as crazy as it seems, because the Bahamas has warm water and great white sharks can't live in warm water. What they have forgotten is that they aren't dealing with your ordinary everyday giant killer great white shark with a grudge. If this shark can place a small log onto a buoy it can jolly well live in warm waters long enough to gobble up the rest of the family. So off the family go, chartering a tiny private plane piloted by Hoagie (Michael Caine), a salty, down-to-earth sort of pilot with street smarts logic but no iron for his shirts, to get them to their destination, a shack-filled shanty town they will now call home. It should be noted that the film contains two love stories for Ellen Brody. The first is the startlingly quick emotional turnaround after the death of her son Sean to thinking about schpoinking Hoagie, and the second is the even more unnatural relationship between her and her son Michael. It's genuinely creepy. So many moments where they look as though they are about to kiss, and so many more of furtive looks and jealous outbursts whenever Hoagie is around her.

A few shark-based nightmares later and Ellen is all settled in to her new home, happy that Michael is safe out on his boat with Jake (Mario Van Peebles) talking to and tagging sea snails. It is here the killer shark proves that not only can it live happily in warm water, but that it has now developed a real taste for boats. Having already eaten Sean's boat, it now tries to chomp its way through Michael's; which must be a special vessel, because it bleeds when it's bitten. Luckily Michael's legs are so long that one push on the seabed sends them hurtling home again. Instead of throwing the idea of living inland into the 'how to stop being continually attacked by sharks' suggestion pot, Michael employs the same rationale that many teenage boys have employed through the years, which is to keep the problem secret from his mum and carry on with his life as if nothing has happened. A choice that, literally, comes back to bite him in the ass a few days later when the shark, once more hankering for some boat nourishment, attacks the tiny underwater Citroen CV that Michael is driving along the seabed. The angry shark, possibly even angrier now because it's having to swim about in warm waters, forces Michael to plunge to safety into a shipwreck, which is conveniently just next to him. Films always seem to find shipwrecks. I have never seen one. Never. And yet bad movies always seem to find them in the most handy of places, just in the nick of time.

Meanwhile, as they are out dancing at a street festival, Hoagie offers a piece of advice to Ellen that would comfort any woman grieving the death of her son, and they are words that I try to live my life by: 'Kick it in the arse, Ellen.' Wise words indeed.

Later on in the film, during an award ceremony for Michael's wife Carla (Karen Young), who has fashioned a giant, red, pointy shark mouth sculpture for the beach, the family decide it would be fine to allow Michael's annoying daughter Thea (Judith Barsi) to go and take a ride on an inflatable banana boat. This is a particularly stupid decision, considering there are only two things they know about this shark: that it likes to eat boats and it likes to eat Brodys. Even though Ellen's supernatural shark spidey sense is tingling, everything is bound to be okay, except that of course it's not going to be okay: there's a bloody great big Brody-boat-loving shark on the loose.

As the banana boat revellers bounce up and down in slow motion – nothing good ever happens in slow motion – up pops the killer shark, and one of the riders seemingly goes and sticks her leg into its mouth. Surely this is no shark attack, this is entrapment. As well as chomping on the attention-seeking woman who was stupid enough to step into it, the shark cannot resist the chance to eat another boat, and now the rest of the gang are hanging on to a deflating piece of plastic as it squirts around the ocean. It is by this point that Ellen, and most of the audience, have just about had enough. After a quick pit-stop to put on her deck-shoes and nautical attire, she steals her son's boat and heads out to face the shark as nature intended, shoulder pads to dorsal fin. Quite what she hopes to achieve is unclear. Maybe she can talk sense into the shark, discuss their differences at a counselling session and part amicably once their conflicts are resolved? Whatever her reasons, the chase is on. And there is double the tension, because there is double the chase: as Ellen is chasing the shark, Hoagie, Michael and Jake are chasing Ellen in Hoagie's little private plane.

When the others eventually find Ellen, Hoagie swoops down from the sky just in time before the growling, snarly shark claims yet another boat. Thus Ellen is saved from impending chompatude. With the plane landed somewhat safely on the water, Michael and Jake make for the boat, but before Hoagie has a chance to charm his way into a glib line, the devilish shark proves that it's not only boats it has a hankering for, it's all modes of transport, and chows down on Hoagie's plane. Sharks may know how to bite things, but they know nothing of a Cockney's resolve. It will take more than a giant shark to defeat Hoagie. Sure enough, moments later, he appears at the side of the boat, throwing insults about the shark's breath; and, despite being thrown into the ocean, he climbs onto the boat completely dry.

The boat is letting in water – I don't know why – so now everybody is stuck in the middle of the ocean with a giant shark holding a grudge. They hatch a plan, and the plan seems to be to point a camera flash at the shark and annoy it for a bit. It's never really explained why they think this will work. Either it's something to do with the explosive device that they want to spear onto the shark, or maybe it has something to do with the shark's intense hatred of the paparazzi; either way, that is how they are going to defeat it. It is also decided that the best way to place the device onto the shark is for Jake to sit on a thin stick poking out of the front of the boat and lean out into the shark. Unfortunately, as Sean learned earlier, leaning into sharks always ends in disaster, and in a few gulps Jake is gone, leaving Michael to let out one long, emotional and cinematic slow-motion 'Nooooooooooooo.'

It is here that the film takes a strange turn, or stranger turn. Michael, now properly pissed off with the shark, stands flashing his device toward the oncoming peril, which breaches and flounces in the water with every burst. 'No pictures, respect my privacy!' the shark seems to growl as each flash goes off. The editing and narrative from this point are kind of 'fill in your own story', as the boat slowly edges toward the shark. Suddenly Ellen remembers the scene from the first *Jaws* movie where Chief Brody utters the immortal words 'Smile, you son of a bitch' (even though she wasn't in that bit, so she must have rented the movie the night before), she remembers the moment when Sean was killed (even though she wasn't in that bit either … I'm starting to think that Ellen and the shark are some weird kind of interspecies Bonnie and Clyde), then the boat pokes the shark with its broken bow and the shark blows up. Yes, that's right, they poke the shark and the shark blows up. I must stress that if you are in a situation where you're being circled by a bloodthirsty great white shark, do not poke it in the hope that it will explode. As far as I know, there is no point on a great white shark that is particularly explosive. The shark blows up, the boat breaks apart and everybody is happy and laughing, surrounded by bits of dead, singed fish flesh. Just as you think it couldn't get any stranger, up pops Jake. A little bloody and with a torn shirt and a nip slip, but alive nonetheless. This supposes that Jake, somehow, managed to hide inside the shark and once the shark exploded was released into the ocean like an underwater human cannon ball. They all then swim to shore holding on to various bits of driftwood, laughing and joking about their lucky escape, and at no point does anybody say, 'Did you see that? We totally just blew up a motherfucking shark. I didn't know sharks could do that, but it totally did. For some reason.' Then again, nobody seems to be noticing that the ocean is lapping up against the sky, either.

The reason for this confused ending is that it was a replacement for one that made even less sense and was considered a bit too gruesome by the film's test audiences. The original had the shark balancing on its back fin like a dolphin as the bow of the boat decapitated it. For some audience members, who were already pretty gipped that Jake had been bumped off, it was a death too far. An alternative ending was devised, but with only a limited budget available, the filmmakers supposedly had to choose between bringing back Mario Van Peebles and finding another shark to destroy in a less gruesome way. The decision was made to bring back Van Peebles, so a new version of the ending was cobbled together incorporating some footage from the ending of the original *Jaws*. It would appear that audiences were fine with this, as was Michael Caine, who reportedly couldn't collect his Oscar win for *Hannah and her Sisters* because he was in a tank at the back of Universal Studios.

Jaws The Revenge is a staple of late-night television and can usually be found on a repeat loop on channels like ITV4. If you have a chance to go and see it on the big screen, I would urge you to do so. Not just so that you can enjoy the bad acting on the big screen but because the 35mm version has some extra footage and uncut scenes, including one part where they accidentally filmed the mechanism that moved the shark along under the water.

Reefer Madness

If 1936 can teach our youth anything, it's the dangers of smoking that terrible weed marijuana. Set against the backdrop of what looks like a 1930s advert for Palmolive soap, *Reefer Madness* (1936), which is also known as *Tell Your Children*, *Dope Addict*, *The Burning Question Doped* and *Doped Youth*, tells the tale of a young man who has the whole world at his feet but whose life is destroyed after he gets involved with the wrong crowd and ends up on trial for murder. All thanks to the demon weed. There aren't many films pre-1975 that I would recommend, but everybody should watch *Reefer Madness* at least once in their life. This film, supposedly made by a church-funded group of filmmakers to serve as a warning to parents, is popular with bad-film audiences because of its wildly inaccurate portrayal of potheads and its even wilder misinformation about the drug itself.

The action opens with some rolling title information about

the horrors we are about to see. It warns that the film may 'startle' you, but it is necessary to help save America's youth from this 'violent narcotic', which is an 'unspeakable scourge' and the 'real public enemy number one'. The real public enemy number one is whoever chose to mix four different fonts on those rolling titles. A lovely bit of nostalgia comes from the old-favourite film effect of the spinning newspaper, followed by a church group meeting for parents about how to win the war on drugs. I wonder if they will ever win that war? They've been fighting it for such a long time now.

The parents are sat in rows, the men wearing suits, the women wearing hats, in what looks like the world's most miserable wedding ceremony, as Dr Square McBuzzkill warns them about how marijuana will kill each and every one of their children. After a short documentary, or what actually looks like some kind of advert for how to make and sell the drug, we are told that greater than the threat of cocaine, pills or heroin is the soul-destroying drug that is marijuana. To prove his point, Dr Square McBuzzkill goes on to tell the story of something that happened in the very city in which they live. How the ungodly and unmarried couple Mae Coleman (Thelma White) and Jack Perry (Carleton Young) ran a marijuana party ring (which sounds like something you'd buy in Iceland at Christmas time) out of an apartment just across the road from the high school. It's like a very polite version of *Breaking Bad*, where everybody wears a suit and has well-combed hair, even at breakfast time.

It is here we meet Ralph (Dave O'Brien). If I may use the language of the time, Ralph is a bounder, a cad of the highest order, who likes to lure teenagers into the apartment and get them hooked on the old Mary Jane. In fact he is going to get Jimmy (Warren McCollum) all mixed up in his nonsense. Poor Jimmy. He's a swell guy, he's got a great family, an amazing girlfriend and a loving sister, but after a few puffs on the devil's seaweed he goes and puts it all into jeopardy when his drugged-up erratic driving causes him to mow down an old man. Actually, 'mow down' is a bit of an exaggeration. A more accurate way to describe it would be that he drives close to an old man, who then slowly falls to the ground. Terrible stunt work aside, the interesting part of this dangerous driving is that Jimmy gets away with it. Smoke a joint and dance to that jazz music and you'll go to hell, but kill a pensioner and you're doing society a favour. He was old and was probably draining the state of money. *Get a job, you old scrounger!*

The kids hang out in a café where the teenagers all look like 40-year-old divorcees. They've got soda pop with straws, they're dancing about to live music and they can sit at tables, chat and smoke like real grown-ups. It is in this café that we meet our first character who is hopped up on the junk; a pianist with the great character name of Hot Fingers Perrone. Not only does Hot Fingers plays swing and jazz like a manic wind-up version of Jools Holland, he also likes to hide in small closets and smoke a strain of marijuana that can turn a man into a cackling Disney villain. His eyes dart about manically as he billows smoke from his twitchy, guffawing face. Maybe all these teenagers are dying from facial cramps and dislocated jaws from the continuous frenzied gurning while smoking, rather than too much of the Devil's herb garden. I am guessing the double speed at which he plays the piano after he's puffed up a storm is where he got his nickname from; or it could be from the fact that he keeps holding his joints by the part that's on fire. I have always lived by my grandmother's adage, 'If it's hot, don't stick your finger in it.' It continues to serve me well. It is also unusual to see a doped-up dude play the shit out of a keyboard in double time, as most of the potheads I know can take up to an hour just trying to figure out how to get the lid up. And by 'getting the lid up', I mean the lid of the piano; it's not street slang for getting an erection. Although now, I guess, it could be.

The real story begins when Jimmy's family and friends become embroiled in one of Mae's sordid pot parties. There's more dancing, but this time there are fewer clothes, and there are kids on the sofas, kissing – yes, that's right, kissing, can you even imagine such a thing? It's poor Bill (Kenneth Craig) that we should feel sorry for. He's been dating Jimmy's sister for some time now; he's carried her books, helped her remember her lines for the school play and enjoys playing doubles tennis. But thanks to the green grass monster, he's not thinking straight and he goes and starts messing around with Mae. Damn those drugs. If they can make a teenager fall for a woman who can't be bothered to clean the house and make the dinner then it really is scrambling their brains. When a 1930s man forgets to scold a woman for not doing her womanly duties, he's in trouble.

In the aftermath of one particularly big gangbang, Mae and Bill have gotten rather amorous, and unbeknownst to Bill, his sweetheart Mary (Dorothy Short) is in the other room, with Ralph. You remember that cad and bounder? Well, now he's living up to his name as he slips Mary a funky cigarette instead of a normal one, and in their drug-fuelled fog tries to fondle her on the sofa and starts to throw her about like a rag doll as he tries to get her dress undone. Our hero, Bill, hearing the screams, runs in, but – *oh no!* – he too is in a marijuana fog, and these advances by Ralph are translated by his brain as Mary offering herself to him on a plate. Bill's not having that, and a laughably-staged fight ensues. Mae's friend Jack brings out a gun, there's a struggle, and *bang!*, Mary is shot dead. And she wasn't old, which is going to make it difficult to brush this one under carpet. They give the gun to Bill, and now he thinks he's killed Mary. The upshot being that now the fuzz have been called and he is going to have to go on trial for murder.

The gang – including Blanche (Lillian Miles), who witnessed the shooting, and Ralph – are going bat-shit crazy being cooped up in the apartment. But they have to keep Ralph indoors – he's a flight risk – so they keep feeding him more and more dope so that he won't squeal to the pigs about what really happened the night Mary bit the big one. Eventually Ralph has had enough – there is only so much piano-playing and chicken sandwiches he can take – so he turns on Jack, killing him by beating him to death. Honestly, where do these potheads get all of this energy from? Luckily for Bill, the gang confess to what really happened that night, and he is off the hook. Hurray! Blanche testifies and then, for some reason, escapes the clutches of the oldest female guardian in the world and jumps out of a window to her death. Remember, this could happen to your children. They too could get stoned, crazy, kill a load of people and then start jumping out of windows. The strangest thing about *Reefer Madness* is that innocent people are killed while the ones who are selling and taking drugs walk away from the film, for the most part, unscathed. If your child starts manically playing the piano, you know what to search their room for. Don't let it happen to you.

Although the film is old and wildly misinformed, there is still a naive charm to it, and the silent-era acting combined with the misrepresentation of the drug for propaganda purposes is a joy to watch. A few friends, a pile of snacks, the recreational poison of your choice, and *Reefer Madness* would make a great night in. Just remember to lock all of the windows and hide all of the guns.

Gigli

Lord only knows what the thinking behind *Gigli* (2003) was. Ben Affleck was great in *Good Will Hunting* (1997) and Jennifer Lopez knocked it out of the park in *Anaconda* (1997) – although that's not difficult when you're acting alongside Owen Wilson, a very lumpy Jon Voight and a CGI snake – so the casting of the leads was not at fault. It was the Year of our Lord 2003 when a lesbian crook, a dumb mobster and a mentally-challenged *Baywatch* enthusiast showed the world how bad a movie could be if it really, really, really tried. The plot of this movie is so basic that if you click the synopsis link on IMDB (at the time of me writing this) it comes up with the message, 'This synopsis is too short and may not include the required detailed description of the entire plot. We normally require that synopses be at least 10 lines long. If you have seen this title, please help us by improving and expanding this synopsis.' The synopsis of the entire plot doesn't even stretch to ten lines; it takes only a dizzying four lines to encapsulate it, and even then I think I could probably do it in one. 'A lesbian and an idiot babysit an autistic stranger for the weekend.' Done.

Affleck plays a guy called Larry Gigli. He is often called Jiggly or Giggly but, as he explains, his surname is actually pronounced 'Gigli, rhymes with really.' Gigli-rhymes-with-really likes to act tough but is actually a soft-hearted sweetie, albeit as dumb as bread. He's been given the task of kidnapping Brian (Justin Bartha), the mentally-challenged brother of a top lawyer, in an attempt to save his gangster boss from being prosecuted. I feel I should stop a moment and talk about Bartha's performance. It's obvious that actors like to employ the method acting approach when assigned roles representing any form of disability. Daniel Day-Lewis spent a lot of time at the Sandymount School Clinic, where he learned about the lives of many disabled people, so that he would be able to remain 'in character' during the filming of *My Left Foot* (1989). Sean Penn visited a Los Angeles jail to research his role of a man with a developmental disability when playing the lead role in *I Am Sam* (2001). For this role in *Gigli*, I imagine Bartha's research method was to watch *Rain Man* (1988) a whole bunch of times on DVD (not just once; that would be lazy) and then wipe his brain of any concept of nuance.

Because Gigli-rhymes-with-really is, as mentioned, as dumb as a loaf of Hovis, his boss sends Ricki (Jennifer Lopez) to make sure he gets the job done. Coming home from his busy day of kidnapping a mentally-challenged guy – something that seems startlingly easy to do (for future reference, you simply have to walk into any mental health hospital or care centre, pick your favourite and casually walk out the door with him/her) – Gigli-rhymes-with-really comes home to find Ricki on his couch. The sexual chemistry between these two actors is almost detectable; her coquettish leg-stretching and low voice coupled with his slack-jawed bovine expression makes for probably one of the greatest meet-cute moments in film history. A scene that is only topped a short while later when Gigli-rhymes-with-really is male-posturing in front of the mirror with a single dumbbell as Ricki reads a book called *Being Peace* in bed. He is the brawn and she is the brains, do you see? How could she resist his muscular body, held in by only the flimsiest of red satin dressing gowns? He is, after all, the bull, and she is the cow. But, as it turns out, the cow is gay. Let's hope nothing stupid happens later in the film that reinforces the idea that homosexuality, especially in women, is a choice that can be overridden because of a simple change of heart. That's what drives sexual identity: perspective.

All three, Ricki, Brian and Gigli-rhymes-with-really, seem happy trapped in this strange *Three's Company* flat-share, but the whole diabolical plot is almost blown wide open with the arrival of Detective Stanley Jacobellis (Christopher Walken) who, with only one small scene, totally steals the movie. Jacobellis is on to them. He's a wise man and he's going to get to the bottom of this case. I think that's what the scene is about. Unfortunately, it seems nobody in the costume department was able to persuade Mr Walken to wear any type of supportive under-garment during the shoot. Very early on in the scene, he takes a high barstool and perches upon it to deliver his speech. This means his swinging sisters are also nestled on top of the stool; and these sisters aren't the shy and retiring type, they are the wild and free and straining-to-be-noticed type. Maybe if he wasn't sitting legs akimbo, my eyes wouldn't be drawn immediately to the large mound that plops on and off the stool like a pair of unruly space hoppers bouncing about in a mail sack (pun totally intended). That's the problem when you notice something in a film; it becomes all you can focus on. Once faced with Walken's unruly, devil-may-care ballbags rolling haphazardly and lawlessly under a sea of khaki trouser, you are never able to forget them. I just thought about them again. Pass the eye-syringe mother, I need some more optic morphine.

The ladies have had the chance to delight in Walken's two veg, and so, for the fellas, there follows a brief yoga session in which Ricki stretches and heaves her skimpy sportswear-attired body about while informing us of her views on male and female genitalia. More films should have scenes like this. *Gone with the Wind* would have been markedly improved by a scene where Rhett Butler gives more of a damn about his balls then about Scarlett O'Hara. Or maybe there should have been an extra song in *The Sound of Music* where children sing of the many words for vagina. 'Hairbags or clamshells or minges or chuffs. Meat wallet, pink canoe, pussy and muff' etc. Ricki goes on to explain that the penis is like a sea slug, or 'a really long toe', which nobody wants to kiss, unlike a mouth, which we learn is the 'twin sister of the vagina'. They must be fraternal twins, because my vagina doesn't have teeth or a tongue, and I don't ever feel the compulsion to shove cake into it – although I am aware that those websites do exist. Okay. Penis = really long toe, vagina = mouth with no teeth. Got it. Thankfully, she stops there and doesn't go on to say, 'The balls are like deflated balloons at a child's birthday party that nobody wants to play with. The tits are like big tennis balls but, you know, less furry and a bit softer. And the ass is … well, don't go near the ass; there be dragons.'

The film can't be all fun, games, scrotums and vagina-championing forever, and soon the Scooby gang are hit with a moral sticky wicket when an order comes through to cut off the thumb of poor Brian. This is a problem, because all Bartha's been doing in the film so far is rocking back and forth staring at his thumb. How is he going to be able to act without it? All this is going to have to wait, as Ricki's ex-lover has turned up, offering a threesome with Gigli-rhymes-with-really in the hope of reviving their relationship; and when she is rejected, she tries to kill herself. Being a lesbian is great, kids, until your crazy ex turns up and casually slits her wrists with a steak knife in front of you. Some people will do almost anything to get out of being in that movie. Fortune smiles on the crazy, though, because the trip to the emergency room means a plan can be hatched; they will sneak into the morgue and snap a finger off a dead guy. It turns out that sneaking into a morgue to play with the corpses is just as easy as sneaking into a sheltered care home to take out one of the patients. I might try both of these next bank holiday Monday.

Thumb posted, it's time for another 'unexpectedly good actor turns up in a really shitty movie' scene as Al Pacino – yes, you saw that right, Al Pacino – appears, playing the oddly camp mob boss Starkman. (Anybody else think that sounds like a naked superhero?) Starkman is unpredictable and a bit pissed off (maybe Narkman would have been a better name) because he knows they've tried to con him with a stranger's thumb. You don't get to the top of the gang crime ladder by not being able to differentiate between thumbs. He's mad and dangerous and trigger-happy, but Ricki's got a plan. Her plan consists of telling Narkman that the thumb idea was stupid and that he is stupid and that his overall scheme is stupid. Like the film is stupid. Luckily, he's too stupid to know when he's being called stupid, so the trio just get up and leave. That's the great thing about mob bosses: they love people squaring up to them and calling them names, and these people are allowed to walk out freely without any fear of reprisals, just like in the real world.

As the film rushes to its disappointing conclusion – yes, this really is the entire plot, and yet it still manages to be two hours long – a new plan is hatched. Instead of just killing poor Brian, whom they have come to like, Ricki and Gigli-rhymes-with-really are going to dump him somewhere and start a new life. As they are driving around, wondering where the best place to dump a naive, mentally disabled, disorientated man might be, they pass a film crew working on a beach scene, and Brian gets overwhelmingly excited thinking they are shooting his favourite show, *Baywatch*. They haven't thought of any better place to dump him, so they literally just leave him there. In one last gesture to prove he's a nice guy, Gigli-rhymes-with-really gives Ricki the keys to his car so that she can get away and 'be all right'.

Brian is happy slow-motion dancing on a beach with scantily-clad women, Ricki is driving to freedom, and poor Gigli-rhymes-with-really is left to reflect on the activities of the past week. The end, right? Not right. Psych! Back rolls Ricki, but her name isn't Ricki, it's Rochelle, and she wants to take Gigli-rhymes-with-really with her, because she's not so much of a lesbian any longer. It's a well-known fact that a cute man giving a woman a car can cure her of being a lesbian.

The major failing is that nothing is really resolved in this film, so I can only guess what happened to the main characters. I am guessing that, after filming the beach scene, Brian dies of starvation, because it turns out that mentally-challenged and institutionalised people aren't so good at suddenly making it on their own; Detective Stanley Jacobellis changes his name to Stan Jacoballs and joins an all-male strip group called Ballz 2 Men; Starkman sets up an anger management programme where he implements his 'get yelled at but don't shoot' approach to organised crime; Ricky and Gigli-rhymes-with-really put their criminal pasts behind them; and all live happily ever after, running a bed and breakfast in Vermont.

Troll 2

Troll 2 (1990) is the sequel to the 1986 film Troll, even though it has absolutely nothing to do with it. Nothing at all. It doesn't even have any trolls in it, which really should be a minimum requirement when calling your film Troll 2. The film is set in a town called Nilbog, and in case you're not Alan Turing, let me crack that mystery code for you: it's just Goblin spelled backwards. What do goblins have to do with trolls? Nothing. Why isn't the town called Sllort? No idea. Perhaps Sllort is a Swedish brand name, or a Norwegian insult meaning the sound a testicle makes when being pulled away from a damp thigh. The real answer to the riddle isn't as inventive: the film was originally going to be titled Goblins, but the studio didn't have much faith in it (I can't see why – apart from the terrible script, acting, sound and story, it's a great film), so they rebranded it Troll 2 in the hope that it might cash in on the minor success of Troll. It's not a very exciting answer; but, to be fair, it isn't a very exciting movie.

It starts innocuously enough with father Michael Waits (George Hardy) taking his family on a vacation to the lovely village of Nilbog on one of those house-swap deals they do televisions shows about. If you can fight your way through the painfully-decorated Waits house and see past the garish fashions of dancing stage-school daughter Holly (Connie

Young) as she thumps un-rhythmically in her room to her youth music, you will start to see a plot emerging ... It is in there, I promise. Holly doesn't want to go on the house-swap trip, as she is upset at the prospect of being parted from her boyfriend, even though she suspects he might be homosexual because he likes to spend time with his friends; Michael is upset because his ungrateful children are moaning about going on holiday; mother Diana (Margo Prey) doesn't appear to mind too much, as she looks absolutely hammered throughout the movie; and son Joshua (Michael Stephenson) is upset because his dead grandfather keeps popping up all over the place telling him not to go on holiday. Grandfather needs to warn Joshua that the people of Nilbog are evil and want to turn everybody into plants and eat them, because they are vegetarians. Even in 1990, the evil nature of vegetarians was being documented on screen. They won't kill a cow, but if they can turn a person into a shrub they will happily stick them in a burger. And don't get me started on the vegans. Bastards, the lot of them.

Of course, Joshua tries to warn his family of the dangers, but his family are too angry, stupid and in one case too drunk to pay any attention. They do what any rational parents would do with a seemingly uncontrollable child: listen careful to what he has to say, then tell him to get in the car and shut the hell up in the back seat. Parents 1, petulant child 0. In a strange and pointless subplot, Elliot (Jason Wright), Holly's boyfriend, has gathered his closest friends, in their shortest short shorts, into an RV and camped just outside the town. He wants to prove to Holly that he will follow her anywhere, even a few hours down the road. The rest of the boys are there for fun. Because nothing says lad's weekend like a Winnebago parked in some scrubland just outside of a weird, Amish-looking town populated by evil vegetarians.

Once the family arrive and swap keys with the family from Grant Wood's *American Gothic* painting, they make their way inside their new home to find a lovely spread of artificially-coloured bright green food waiting for them – and we all know how appetising bright green food is. It is the colour of all the best foods; absinthe, unripe bananas, Listerine. Never knowing when to stay dead, Grandpa Seth turns up again to warn Joshua of the dangers of eating the green food. Maybe he should have turned up in pre-production and warned the family about the dangers of starring in a film so bad that the food is capable of out-acting the cast. Joshua has to stop them eating the food, but how? He could scream, he could pretend to faint, he could pull the tablecloth from under it – but that might result in accidentally doing that trick where the tablecloth comes away without disturbing the food, leaving the poisoned food intact and ready for consumption. Ultimately Joshua does what any sane little boy does when he doesn't want anybody touching his stuff; he stands on the table and urinates all over everything. Again: he stands on the table and *urinates* over the food. A person wrote that into a scene; a person with a family and a functioning brain, a person who thinks that a child weeing onto green buns is really going to get them noticed in the film industry. I mean, it has, but for all the wrong reasons.

A furious father carries Joshua to his room and yells one of the film's most popular lines, 'You can't piss on hospitality!' Throwing him on the bed, the dad struggles with his belt. Joshua, and the audience, may be concerned that his father is going to beat him with the belt. I was hoping he was going to get his long toe out and piss on Joshua in an act of retribution. Unfortunately it's a joke: he is going to have to tighten his belt, because piss-soaked green-covered buns are not an appropriate foodstuff, no matter how hungry you are.

Back to the lads in the RV. The nerdiest lad, Arnold, played by Darren Ewing, one of the few actors here who actually went on to do some proper acting, decides to go for a stroll to check out what the scratch of woodland they are parked on has to offer. It turns out that what it has to offer is an attractive young girl being chased by a pack of evil-looking goblins – I mean trolls – or is it goblins? Regardless of the film's title, I'm just going to call them goblins. Most of the goblins are short, with grotesque faces and buggy eyes, and all of them have their own weapons. All, that is, apart from one, whom I have affectionately named Lefty. Poor Lefty is obviously the runt of the goblin litter. He walks a little slower, his buggy eyes are a little buggier, and the only weapon he is allowed to carry is a small pointy stick. But he's still part of the pack, and the pack is chasing down this damsel in distress. Luckily for her, Arnold the nerd is there to save her, or at least run into her, scream like a tiny child and get stabbed in the shoulder by a goblin with a makeshift spear – the kind of spear that Lefty could only dream of wielding. Fleeing for their lives, they enter a strange chapel occupied by an even stranger witch who, it turns out, is Queen of the Goblins. There was a girl in my school who had the same nickname; as I recall, she was very popular with the boys. This Queen of the Goblins isn't as nice a person. Quick as a flash, she melts the fleeing girl into a delicious green gloop that is now ripe green food for the goblins, and then she attacks poor Arnold and turns him into a tree. Why has she done this? I ... It could be ... There's that ... I have no idea.

Meanwhile, in the sleepy psycho village of the damned vegetarians, Joshua is prannying about and playing amateur detective by trying to find more information with which to convince his family that perhaps an Amityville house of horrors in Nilbog isn't such a great holiday destination. He sneaks up into the rafters during what looks like the Manson Family's church service, where the crazy-faced locals (seriously, there must be at least fifty people in that church and not *one* eye is pointing in the same direction) are being preached to about the dangers of eating meat and the malevolent personalities of those who would put a dead animal into their bodies. Once again, killing humans and turning them into plants in order to eat them is totally fine, but as soon as you pop a chicken nugget into your mouth, you are a monster. A *monster*! But I've seen vegetarians eating figs and, as we all know, in the centre of *every* fig is a digested wasp. (That's a true fact, by the way.) Not even I would eat that, and I've eaten a kebab bought from the back of a moped. Of course, Joshua can't do anything right, and he gets caught and surrounded by these goon-faced laughing yokels, who try to force-feed him eyeball ice cream. I know it sounds as though I'm making it all up but, unfortunately, I'm not. His father follows his cries and runs in, ever the hero; and when confronted by an angry mob force-feeding his son, he does what every parent would do in that situation: he looks a bit suspicious and then yells at his son for causing trouble, before taking him home. Kids. If they're not bleeding you dry and asking for PlayStations, they're out becoming the target of a vegetarian goblin-based diet.

All might be better now, as it seems the townsfolk have had a change of heart and are sorry for trying to force-feed the Waits boy human-body-parts ice cream. By way of an apology, they have decided to throw them all a lovely party. The blind, stupid and drunk members of the family are thrilled, but Joshua is not having it; he doesn't trust them. He's right to be suspicious, as the 'party' is nothing more than a bunch of pudding-faced Nilbog inhabitants encircling the awkward-looking family, clapping and humming along to their favourite song. |I think the song is called, 'Do dododododonananananana, let's make everybody feel as uncomfortable as possible and then turn them into plants and eat them.' Off trots Joshua to find and talk to Grandpa Seth, who still refuses to stay dead. Instead, Joshua finds the Queen of the Goblins, who turns into a goblin and jumps through a mirror to attack him. But, not to worry, somehow Grandpa Seth is back, and now armed with an axe, and he quickly Luke-Skywalkers the goblin's hand clean off. Sure, a dead guy with an axe is handy, but a dead guy with a Molotov cocktail is even handier, so Joshua takes one that his Grandpa just happens to have and throws it at the preacher, setting him on fire. Goblins aside, this is one troubled kid. Pissing on food and setting fire to strangers is not acceptable behaviour; somebody should teach him that. Luckily a conviction for attempted murder is avoided, because the man isn't a man at all; he's a goblin in a man suit, who quickly turns into a barbecued dead goblin. The goblins are angry. Cooking a vegetarian is the height of disrespect, and Lefty leads the charge against the murderers by waving his small stick around aggressively (well, as aggressively as you can wave a small stick).

The Queen is still a bit annoyed about her missing hand, so

she returns to her chapel where she sticks her stump into the Stone-a-matic 3000 Grow Your Own Hand Machine and – *kapow!* – all of her appendages are returned to normal. Not wanting her spanky new hand to look out of place on her old crone body, she then shoves her entire face and body into the machine, and is transformed into one of those sexy ladies with the big hair who were very popular in films of the early 1990s. This Queen of the Goblins is much more attractive now that she's standing up straighter and has fewer herpes scabs all over her mouth. I am now going to tell you exactly what happens next. You won't believe me, but I swear it is all true. So, until you witness it for yourself, you're going to have to trust me. This is why I recommend you go and see this film, even if it's just to see how *not* to make a movie. The now sexy Queen of the Goblins approaches the RV (remember the RV with the nerds inside) where Brent (David McConnell), the only friend who isn't dead or surrounded by goblins, is residing. Things get a little steamy, they get comfy together, they exchange furtive looks, and then they start eating corn on the cob, sexily, on the bed, like Lady and the Tramp but with corn not spaghetti and in a beige caravan. As they munch each other's corn – not a euphemism – the RV starts to fill with exploding pockets of popcorn. The popcorn keeps popping all over the place, buckets of it, filling the RV and drowning poor Brent. And then the scene ends. That's it. I don't know what audiences were supposed to take away from that. I don't know why Brent and the Queen are eating corn, and I don't know why they get covered in a ton of exploding popcorn. I don't know what the popcorn is supposed to symbolise. The internet tells me that if you dream of popcorn it means new ideas and collaborations that will be fruitful. But that can't be it; the guy dies. Unless that was his new idea. What I do know is that I don't want to be sat in a cinema next to the guy who wrote that scene; he clearly has a weird, sexual popcorn fetish.

Meanwhile, back at Nilbog central, the family has a quick séance to try to bring Grandpa Seth, back even though he hasn't stopped coming back since the film started. The spiritual hook-up works, which means, for some reason, that Grandpa can be mortal for ten minutes. Don't over think that bit; you'll go mad. In that ten minutes, Grandpa hands Joshua a super-secret goblin-killing weapon concealed in a paper bag. As the family try to fight off angry goblins, Joshua and the now mortal Grandpa Seth set about trying to destroy the goblin world from the chapel of the Queen, who has returned from her popcorn adventure with her goblin army. But let us not forget that Joshua has that super-secret weapon. What could, technically, be called a fight breaks out, and Joshua decides to break out the brown paper bag revealing the weapon, which turns out to be a double-decker baloney sandwich. He takes a big bite and goblins start falling down all over the place. It would seem that all it takes for the family to vanquish the goblin veggies is a bit of processed meat in white bread. *White bread!* The devil's loaf. Sandwich eaten, goblins destroyed by the power of spam, it's time to head home again, adventure over. Or is it? It would seem those tricksy goblins, immune to the harmful nature of tubed meat, have pre-empted the family's arrival and filled the fridge with delicious green food. The film ends with Joshua rushing in to find his dead mother being eaten by goblins; but I'm sure it's nothing that a quick trip to McDonald's won't solve. We'll never find out, though, because the film, like many *good* bad movies, just ends. No explanations, no tying up of loose ends, just the making of more loose ends to dangle away in infinity. I just hope that Lefty, eventually, found love. Or at the very least, a bigger stick.

Showgirls

A popular late-night bad film treat, *Showgirls* (1995) tells the story of Nomi Malone (Elizabeth Berkley), a sassy woman who opens the action hitching a ride to Vegas with a potential rapist. As film openings go, it's a bold move to start with a possible rape. Thankfully Nomi always carries a knife with her, and seeing that this gal is no pushover makes the guy rethink his plan to commit a serious sexual assault. So then they continue their ride toward Nevada. I imagine there's nothing more comfortable than a six-hour drive with a man who has already tried to rape you. There would be so much to talk about.

'Remember that time back there when you tried to rape me?'
'Yeah. Remember when I threatened to stab you with my knife?'
'Yeah.'
'Those were some fun times.'

Putting their differences aside, they get to Vegas and stop off to do a bit of gambling. Nomi has left her bag containing all her worldly possessions in the truck – the truck that belongs to the man who has already shown signs of a serious lack of concern for acceptable public behaviour, so I'm sure her things will be safe. When it finally dawns on poor Nomi that her bag is *not* safe, and that she has lost everything, she runs to the car park and starts to take her anger out on a parked car. A bit like Basil Fawlty in that episode of *Fawlty Towers*, but with more hair and bigger boobs. When the owner of the car, Molly (Gina Ravera), returns to find her vehicle being assaulted, she does what every sane and logical human would do in that situation: she takes Nomi out for a spot of dinner. It puts me in mind of the time when my car was stolen from outside my house and the police caught the guy because he went through a red light and crashed into a taxi while drunk. He totalled my lovely car, and I remember it took all of my inner strength not to ask him over for a lasagne.

After dinner, Molly could just send Nomi on her merry way. Nobody would judge her; she's already done more than most people would in that situation. But that is the sort of thing that happens in a film that makes sense. This is *Showgirls*. Instead, she asks if Nomi would like to come and live with her. It would seem that Molly was on the lookout for a crazy, knife-carrying, car-smashing stranger to share her life with. This is Vegas, after all, and Molly certainly hit the jackpot in finding the perfect unpredictable loon. Bear in mind that this has all happened in the first nine minutes of a 128-minute film. Perhaps director Paul Verhoeven wasn't that confident in audiences making it to the end of the movie, so he put most of the plot in the first half-hour and coasted for the rest. The girls move in together; in this household, Nomi does the stripping and Molly makes the costumes. Perfect.

Later, a rivalry is sparked when Nomi meets Cristal Connors (Gina Gershon), who is headlining the high-budget show *Goddess* at the Stardust Casino. Cristal thinks of herself as an artist and sees *Goddess* as more of an art show than just titillation. It is far superior to the other topless dancing shows at the less glamorous and, probably, stickier boobie joints in Vegas. Cristal is not impressed to find out that Nomi is working at Cheetah's Topless Club. She even goes as far as to call Nomi's job little more than prostitution. The catty name-calling scenes are where you will find the best kind of eyebrow overacting in this movie; the eyebrows dance and gesture like caterpillars twirling on a hot branch. Sadly female eyebrow overacting is a dying art, as more and more turn to paralysing their faces with Botox, rendering the eyebrow sad and inanimate. Both women exchange pointed glances and lip snarls and then walk off in a huff.

A real lip-gloss David-and-Goliath competitiveness forms between the two of them, which is reminiscent of any sequined, shoulder-padded plot from a 1980s American soap opera. With evil oozing out of her, Cristal sends Nomi on what is supposedly a PR job but is actually an escort assignment. In an oddly twisted move, Cristal then turns up at Nomi's work and pays her to give her boyfriend Zack (Kyle MacLachlan) a lap dance. I say lap dance; it's really no more than a naked woman violently bouncing about on poor Kyle MacLachlan's penis. She leaps about on it as if he were a bouncy castle. I don't have a penis, so I'm not an expert on how to maintain one, but surely squatting on it from a reasonable height and then aggressively bashing it with a pubic bone can't be good for it. If you think the lap dance is awkward, you might want to fast-forward through the sex-having scene in the swimming pool, which perfectly recreates a dolphin display at a SeaWorld where somebody has snuck LSD into the fish food. Nomi wraps herself around Zack and splashes and whips her hair about like a washing machine drum making a break for freedom. She twists and grinds and splashes and spins as though her vagina is plugged into an electric whisk. Again, it's poor MacLachlan's penis I feel most sorry for.

Nomi's revenge for all of the prostitution, name-calling and backbiting is to audition for a part in Cristal's show *Goddess*, work hard at her dancing skills, become more popular and more powerful, take Cristal's boyfriend and then steal her place in the spotlight. But gosh-darn that Cristal, she goes and throws a spanner in the works by threatening to sue the casino if Nomi is hired. So the offer of a part in *Goddess* is withdrawn. Nomi could contact a lawyer, go to the press with a tell-all exclusive, slowly befriend Cristal until she gives her a part – or she could just shove Cristal down the stairs, don her still-warm costume and go out there and dazzle her way into stardom, which is exactly what she does.

A chunk of plot and back-story all seems to happen at once and within the space of twenty minutes. There are a few violent beatings, the rape of Nomi's best friend, a cover-up of assault and the revelation of Nomi's secret past involving prostitution and crime coupled with an unstable upbringing. The more popular Nomi becomes, the more she is investigated, and it is revealed that her father shot her mother and then himself; so she got the hell out of dodge with a plan to show her boobs to as many tourists as she could in Vegas. It's all too much. Nomi decides she has had enough – fame and fortune and glittery nipple stickers are not for her – so she quits the big-time boob show. As an audience member sitting through the movie, I know exactly how she feels; if I could have quit watching the movie, I would have, especially after the 'ass-jackhammer on defenceless penis' strip club scene. Off Nomi saunters to make up with Cristal, who is apparently fine with having been pushed down the stairs and never being able to work again. She likes the easy life of not having to fetch things, and is now able to laze about all day on the sofa. She's also spending her lawsuit money on chocolate and even shinier dressing gowns. Nomi then makes a stop to beat up the guy who raped her friend (which proves remarkably easy), then starts hitching a ride back to LA.

What are the chances of her getting a lift with the same fast-talking, sexually amoral truck driver from the start of the film? Apparently the odds are 1-1. Oh, how they will probably laugh together as they talk about the last time they met and he tried to attack her and then stole all of her stuff. Off they drive into the distance toward LA, and into an uncertain and wholly unsatisfying ending. But it *is* an ending, and for that we can be grateful.

This film has that *Beyond the Valley of the Dolls* (1970) appeal and is so outrageously camp and sparkly that you can't help but enjoy it. Even though it was a flop twice – once on its original release, and then again when they rereleased it using a more camp marketing strategy after it collected a slew of Razzie awards. It's got heart and it's got balls, but it's got no plot; and, really, no amount of boobs are going to distract you from that fact.

3
How to Safely Watch
A Bad Movie

You might think that settling down to watch a bad movie is just the same as gearing up to watch any other kind of movie, but you'd be wrong. Much like piloting an aircraft or performing major heart surgery, there are skills that must be learned, knowledge that must be gained and a number of health and safety matters that must be taken into consideration. There are also a number of unwritten rules and regulations, which I am, helpfully, now committing to paper, that should be adhered to when attempting to watch a bad movie. These rules are needed to ensure the experience of watching a bad movie isn't going to cause any lasting damage. You may choose to forego my sage advice, but be warned, many a horror story is told of those who seek out the badness for fun.

For example, there was once a boy in Durham who didn't heed the warnings and laughed in the face of those who spoke of bad-movie dangers. Legend has it that upon his attempt to watch *Catwoman* (2004), unaccompanied, his body shut down every single one of his vital organs and scrambled his brain so badly that he said only the sentence 'Cats come when they feel like it, not when they're told' over and over again until he died. So before you press play on that DVD, VHS or pay-per-view movie, ask yourself if you are willing to put your family through the pain, trauma and embarrassment of explaining that the last moment of your life was spent watching Halle Berry and Sharon Stone trying to act their way out of a kitty-litter bag.

Know what you're letting yourself in for

The first and most important factor to take into consideration is, you *must* know beforehand that the film you are about to watch is a bad one. Never allow a bad film just to sneak up on you; they are dangerous predators that will steal your time along with your will to live if you are not ready for them. Imagine driving a minibus full of seven-year-old girls whom you have told are off for a fun day at Peppa Pig World, then imagine stopping that minibus at Reading Services to tell them that, actually, they are all off to the orthodontist's to get braces and root canals. Can you picture the carnage? The crying, the screaming, the tremendous tantrums and the unrelenting ear-piercing screams. That is how a human brain reacts when you tell it you are going to the cinema to see a comedy and you end up watching *Son of the Mask* (2005). Nothing turns a brain to mush quicker than giving it *Jack and Jill* (2011) when it's expecting *21 Jump Street* (2012).

You should try to acclimatise your brain during the days leading up to your bad-movie-watching experience by getting it into training. Watch some low-quality television programmes like *The Derbyshire Community News Channel*, *Pottery Today*, or any of the output from ITV4. Find clips of bad acting – any Australian soap opera from the 1980s should be fine – and whenever you stumble across something good, slap yourself in the face. Also see if you can find some examples of bad accent acting. Don't just go for the classic Dick Van Dyke option; seek out more contemporary examples, like Don Cheadle's British accent in *Oceans 11* (2001) or Tom Cruise's butchering of the Irish accent in *Far and Away* (2007). That way, when you are confronted with a geographically-challenged accent, or talent-challenged acting, it won't faze you.

Never attempt more than four bad movies in a row, and never go straight in with a grade 10 bad movie like *Stripped to Kill II: Live Girls* (1989) or *Sex Lives of the Potato Men* (2004); these films are far too pure for a novice and could kill you in a heartbeat. Again, ease yourself in gently, by watching something like *The Proposal* (2009) with a group of friends, and gradually work your way up.

Have someone with you

You should never be alone when watching a bad movie. This is the most important rule of all. Sitting by yourself, regardless of the location, while watching a bad movie can be utterly depressing. Suddenly the room feels bigger and emptier, and even a little colder. You rapidly become aware of the futility of existence, and experience a creeping sense of disillusionment and ennui. After all, if society can allow a film like *Year One* (2009) to be made, then it can allow anything: mass genocide; the fundamental breakdown of previously-held ideologies; or, even worse, a sequel – *Year Two*. (Don't panic, there is no sequel, I checked.)

When watching a bad movie, you need people around you, for a number of reasons. For a start, if the movie is so bad that it begins to scar you mentally – I still get *Norbit* (2007) flashbacks – then at least there are people readily available to offer hugs, tea and emotional support. You could be in a living-room or in a movie theatre or on a coach trip around Europe; it doesn't matter where you are, there simply have to be others experiencing the movie with you. You also need a spotter to double-check that you *are* actually seeing the preposterousness on the screen and that you haven't lapsed into a temporary hallucinogenic state. These people can validate that, yes, the makers of *Exorcist: The Beginning* (2004) really do expect you to believe that that hyena is real, or that, no, it's not just you, everybody can see that Sharon Stone's nipples are pointing in different directions in *Basic Instinct 2* (2006).

It is also important to have company so that you have somebody to share moments of absurdity with; somebody to laugh at the super-serious bits with, so you know you are not the only one who finds what they are watching laughably ridiculous. You need somebody to share glances of disbelief with and be there with you to rewind the film and make doubly sure that John Barrowman actually did just say what you think he just said. It could be a small group of friends, a single like-minded pal or a massive gang of film fans off to tolerate a showing of *Howard the Duck* (1986). No matter who you go with, your aim is to get everybody laughing and enjoying the experience. Company during adversity can be a real soul-lifter.

A side note to this. It is extremely important that the people you are taking with you also know they are about to watch a bad movie. The only thing more dangerous than attempting to watch a bad movie on your own is watching one with others who think they are going to see a regular movie or, worse still, a *good* movie. Instead of the uplifting shared experience of getting through a shit film together, you will create a feeling of menace and foreboding, not to mention some really angry friends who might never speak to you again. Going back to the analogy of the minibus full of seven-year-old girls and Peppa Pig World, imagine that after telling them about the change of plans and creating abject misery you then abandoned them at the orthodontist's office, and the orthodontist had no clue that they were coming. In that scenario the kids *and* the orthodontist are served with unpleasant surprises that are guaranteed to ruin their day, and everybody hates you. Forever.

It is also important to be familiar with your surroundings. If you are going to the cinema, make a note of the emergency exits, just in case you start to yawn so much with boredom that you become dizzy and disorientated – even more so than from just watching the movie. Plan an escape route, chose an aisle seat, and time how long it takes you to get from your seat to the car-park or concession stand. When you start to panic during the movie, the knowledge that you have planned a quick escape will soothe you. If watching a DVD at a friend's house, ensure he or she is the kind of friend who wouldn't mind seeing you throw up in front of them or who will stroke your hair if you start screaming for no apparent reason. At home, you should surround yourself with objects of comfort; your favourite blanket, a stuffed animal, copious amounts of vodka, whatever you need to make you feel safe. Never watch a bad movie at your grandmother's house; the patterned carpets and wall-to-wall knickknacks on top of the crap emanating from the television may over stimulated your brain and cause it to shut down completely.

Avoid close-to-home subjects

Another helpful tip when watching bad movies is to avoid, if you can, those that feature characters working within the same occupation as you. Watching a bad actor talk bad science while fiddling about with bubbling beakers or microscopes, trying to say things like 'density-gradient centrifugation' or 'nuclear magnetic resonance spectroscopy' (thank you internet), may make an actual scientist want to start throwing objects at the screen. This doesn't have to apply only to your job; it could be your hobby or just a subject you happen to know something about. For example, I have a friend with an interest in meteorology – nothing on a professional level, but he loves studying weather patterns and things like that – and I made the mistake of inviting him over and showing him the climate-change disaster movie *The Day After Tomorrow* (2004). Climate change being one of the areas he was most interested in, he was already geared up to hate the movie. He was also annoyed with me because I'd told him we were going to watch *Harry Potter and the Philosopher's Stone* (2001). If you've seen it yourself (*The Day After Tomorrow*, not *Harry Potter and the Philosopher's Stone*), you will know that it offers plenty of things to get annoyed about, including the way knowledge is treated with the burning books scenes, and the needless romantic and bromantic subplots. Then there is the particularly idiotic scene where angsty Sam Hall (Jake Gyllenhaal), on encountering a locked door to a pharmacy on board a ship that has sailed down the streets of Manhattan, takes an emergency fire axe, climbs out onto a ledge, being careful to avoid the angry wolves (*shrug*), breaks the pharmacy window, climbs in and unlocks the door from the inside. The scene is obviously there to create a bit of tension, but all I think when I see it is, *Why didn't he just use the fire axe to break the door down? Presumably that is what the fire axe is there for.*

Hall's misunderstanding of axes, however, was not what annoyed my friend. Nor was it the insanity of the plot, nor the terrible acting, nor the fact that the filmmakers seem to have believed that a fast-moving frost can be stopped in its tracks by a library door. All of that he was fine with. What really got to him was the bit near the end of the film where it reaches its most factually inaccurate conclusion, as the temperature drops to something like 130 degrees below zero and all of Manhattan starts to freeze over – apart from the library door, as mentioned just now; it's made of magic heat. As we watched the big freeze take over the city – an impressive special effect for the time – he completely lost his composure and started yelling at the television screen, 'You should be dead! You should all be dead!' He then started pointing at characters individually, 'You should be dead, and you should be dead, and you should be dead!' He then huffily took a piece of pizza, opened a can of beer and sat back sulking in his chair, still muttering and tutting. He was too close to the 'science', and he knew that at 130 degrees below zero, the ice forming from the water that was covering everything should have been doing what ice has always done, expand. Anybody who has put a can of soda in the freezer to 'chill for a few minutes' and then forgotten about it, only to hear a muffled bang and then open the freezer to find it covered in Coca-Cola snow, will know what happens when frozen water expands. That ice should have been crushing buildings and people and cars, and even those huddled behind the library door, I don't care how magic it is; and my friend thought the filmmakers should have shown that. But everybody being crushed to death by expanding ice wouldn't have made for that feel-good-factor Hollywood happy ending. My buddy had to realise that, in the movies, science is literally more fiction than fact. These same frustrations must be experienced by anybody who works as a computer programmer having to watch *Hackers* (1995) or *Independence Day* (1996), or by any astrophysicist sitting through *Armageddon* (1998) or *Deep Impact* (1998).

The easiest way to avoid inadvertently seeing a movie that clashes with your hobby or job is to carefully read the back of the DVD cover or scrutinise the front cover artwork. If it has a picture of space, binary code or a character wearing uniform while crossing his arms and leaning on something, it's probably best to avoid it.

You might also find it handy to know that the occupations most commonly found in the plots of bad movies, and so the most likely to be fudged, glossed over or just made up are: biologist, physicist, computer hacker/programmer, doctor, meteorologist, engineer, weapons expert and pilot. I would have included shark hunter, but if you have a job that awesome, why would you bother leaving the ocean to watch a shitty movie?

Work hard on suspending disbelief

Which leads us on neatly to the next point: suspending disbelief. We all have to buy into the movies we watch, be a bit forgiving of improbabilities and give them a little reality wiggle-room. We know that Superman can't fly (and, more importantly, doesn't exist), that aliens are not coming down to attack us from Mars, and that now and then we may have to sit through Lindsay Lohan's acting. Yet we accept all of these things in order for us to immerse ourselves in the movie experience. But, with a bad movie, you have to suspend your disbelief a very long way, and I mean a Felix Baumgartner distance. (You know, the dude who did a freefall from the edge of space but also has a name that sounds like Bum Gardener.)

It's not just the acting and the special effects that you have to account for, it's the ridiculous storylines, the obvious day-for-night shoots and location swaps. *Shark Attack 3* (2002) is supposedly set in Mexico, in a resort where every background extra is beautiful and permanently grinning or splashing about in the sunshine – which is odd, because this Mexico looks uncannily like Bulgaria. The glut of Eastern European actors who are badly dubbed by bad actors doing bad Mexican accents only confirms that the setting is more Plovdiv than Playa del Carmen.

As with all shark movies or movies that feature an ocean-dwelling killer – squid, whale, jellyfish, crab with a flick-knife – the main characters' decision to stay put and fight is something we have to blindly accept. I live by the sea and I love it; I love seeing the ocean in the morning and having the cool breeze waft gently though the open windows in the summertime. But if I ever got even a whiff of a zombie stingray or a military-mutated cockle killing machine, I'd be off. The answer to the question, 'Why are the military spending all of that money on creating mutant killer cockles when they already have nuclear weapons?' is, of course, 'Shut up.' Common sense dictates that if characters don't want to be killed in their sleep by a giant squid, they should move inland; we all know this, but we have to accept their decision needlessly to continue living next to a killer. Plus, if they didn't, then films like *Jaws* (1975) or *Piranha 2: The Spawning* (1981) would last only a few minutes.

Sustenance is your friend

Food will help you through the onslaught of whatever film nonsense is thrown at you, so it's a good idea to keep a steady supply of snacks to hand when you're watching a terrible movie. Popcorn, hot dogs and nachos are all ideal fare when you're engrossed in a good movie; they are just something to keep your hands busy, and they make no loud crinkling or popping noises that could cause a distraction. The reverse is true with a bad movie. Here it is the snacks' mission to act as a distraction. If your brain becomes too engaged with the plotline of a film like *The Rock* (1996), and tries to make sense of that heady mix of kidnapping, poison gas and Nicholas Cage, it will begin to break down. An exciting snack like a jalapeño-infused cheese dip with extra onions, with its peppery hot goodness, is going to be a delicious and fiery distraction for your body, and last just long enough for your brain to kick back into action.

As well as distracting you, snacks like this can help keep you awake. Say, for example, you're having to watch a film like *You've Got Mail* (1998), and it's so dull that it's literally making you fall asleep in your chair; a bucket full of Tunnock's Teacakes or maybe twelve to fifteen Mars bars should keep your sugar levels buzzing long enough for you to get to the end of the movie. It should also give you the sudden boost you need to delete it from your collection or eject the film from your DVD player so that it can be destroyed and no other human in your house will have to endure that kind of pain and suffering again. I would recommend staying away from heavy, starchy foods such as pizza and chips. Snarfing these down will only make you feel full and sleepy, and you don't need to give your body more of an excuse to make you hunker down for a quick snooze. *Batman and Robin* (1997) will be more than happy to do that for you. Relax and let the slowest and dullest comic-book movie wash over you as your body comfortably slows to accommodate all of the mashed potato you've eaten. A truly deadly mix.

What I like to do is try to match my snacks to the movie I'm watching; but not in too obvious a way like having flying saucer sweets for a sci-fi movie or pastel-coloured cupcakes for some godforsaken romantic comedy. No, I like my snacks to be a bit more esoteric. If I'm watching *Zombie Lake* (1981), for example, I'll make myself pork burgers with a Christmas-spiced apple chutney. Christmas spice makes me think of Germany, which is pertinent because the zombies in the lake are Nazi soldier corpses left over from the war, and pork is said to be the type of meat most similar to human flesh, which is what zombies eat. Hence pork burgers with Christmas-spiced apple chutney. I also put a little bit of cayenne pepper in the mix, just to keep my mouth interested, so that my face doesn't lapse into a boredom coma or try to work out why the green from the zombie 'flesh' is rubbing off onto the face of a topless Italian woman.

Another of my favourites goes well with the Nicholas Cage version of *The Wicker Man* (2006). For watching this movie, I make individual honey loaf cakes and cover them with burned caramel frosting. I then play a game, the rule of which is that whenever Nicolas Cage says either 'burned' or 'honey', I shove a cake in my face. I've almost choked to death twice during the now infamous scorched doll scene that sees Cage yelling the phrase 'How'd it get burned? How'd it get burned?' over and over and over again. There is also enough sugar in the frosting to keep me going at least to the part where he pushes a woman while dressed like a bear.

I like to think I can conjure up a snack to match any bad movie. Pea risotto for *Snowbeast* (1977), spicy chicken wings for *Road House* (1989), or how about spinach gnocchi for *Troll 2* (1990)? Maybe I'll write a cookery book on how to match the best snacks to the worst movies, and I'll call it *'Lights, Camera, Snacktion'*. (I am *totally* going to write that book next.)

Once you have your snacks sorted, it's time to bring out the best type of friend you can have with you while watching a movie travesty. Booze. Copious amounts of delicious alcohol will help increase your tolerance level and make you more accepting of the obviously-flawed narrative. Of course you can theme your alcohol to your bad movie too. A few Cosmopolitan cocktails are good if you are going to sit through *Sex and the City 2* (2010); but for getting a person through a film like *Under Siege 2: Dark Territory* (1995) or *Cobra* (1986), you can't beat a nice, ice cold beer ... or fifteen ... and a couple of Jagerbombs.

There are actually two ways in which beer can facilitate getting thorough a bad movie. First, the steady sipping and slipping into an unconscious beery state is one way; there is no doubt that beer can help numb the effects of watching something painful, like Paris Hilton's acting in *The Hottie& the Nottie* (2008). Secondly, thanks to beer's effect on the human body, the viewer will also be forced into making frequent trips to the bathroom, thus breaking up the 'action' into bladder-relieving manageable chunks. Be warned, however: alcohol can sometimes stave off the effects of a bad movie while you are watching, but the following morning you could be left with a bad-movie hangover, which is the worst kind of hangover imaginable. Not only will you feel like Boogaloo Shrimp is dancing the finale of *Breakin' 2: Electric Boogaloo* (1984) in your head, your tongue will feel as hairy as the Yeti in *Abominable Snowman* (2013), and you will also have to deal with flashbacks from the previous evening's crappy film. Imagine kneeling on the floor of your bathroom with your head down the toilet throwing up a mixture of beer and Tunnock's Teacakes and, on top of that, having the sex scene from *The Matrix Reloaded* (2003) keep popping into your brain. Being sick is bad enough without having to deal with the repeated image of Keanu Reeves' ass bobbing along to a kettle drum techno music soundtrack.

Keep track of time

One of the more fascinating side effects to keep in mind when preparing to watch a bad movie is the change it causes in the perception of time. We all know that just as one person will experience time flying during a particular event, another will experience time dragging. For example, when my lovely, but super nerdy, boyfriend persuaded me to go and see *Superman: Man of Steel* (2013) in the cinema, he sat watching with a massive grin on his face from beginning to end and was genuinely disappointed when the closing credits appeared. (For him, though, that is never the 'end' of the movie; he is that guy who will sit there and read all of the credits, and I've had ushers sweeping under him during the changeover because he refuses to move.) For him, time had zipped along like a giggling child playing in a corn field as he watched the Man of Steel embracing his powers and thwarting bad guys. Can I ask, why do we even need another origin story for Superman? If people don't already know how Superman became Superman, or Spiderman became Spiderman, then maybe being outside with normal folk isn't for them? For me, however, that dumb-ass movie seemed to stop time completely. Each minute seemed to last an hour, and even three trips to the concession stand didn't keep my brain engaged with reality long enough for me to hang on to a simple thought or complete a simple task. I even stuck my hand through the plastic lid of my Pepsi cup thinking it was my popcorn. True story. The official term coined for this phenomenon is 'temporal illusion'.

71

Hold on tight now, here comes the science (and I mean actual science, not bad-movie science-ish). Temporal illusion occurs when there is a distortion in a person's perception of time for a variety of reasons. For my boyfriend, the film's running time was misperceived not as two hours and twenty-three minutes, but as only half that. For me, the running time was misperceived as an entire bank holiday weekend.

This kind of kink in an individual's time perception is why it is necessary for bad movies to keep their running time to a maximum of 100 minutes; and for the most part they do, with most coming in at between 86 and 95 minutes. Any bad movie longer than that could cause a major misperception of time; that is to say, a person who is watching the director's cut of *The Swarm* (1978) might have cause to celebrate a birthday during it, believing that a year of their life has passed as they sit and watch Michael Cain constantly yammering on about bees.

Remain hopeful

Lastly, it is important to remember that the negative effects a bad movie has on the body are only temporary. The feeling of euphoria and relief that will flood your system when the movie ends can quickly be overtaken by a foreboding sense of nonspecific dread at the thought of having to relive any of those cinematic moments again. This is what I like to call post cinematic stress disorder. Just as the perception of time becomes confused while watching a bad movie, there too is an effect on memory. From empirical studies conducted at the various live shows we have been doing with the Bad Film Club over the past ten years, it would appear that very quickly after the end credits have rolled, the brain begins to erase the memory of a bad movie from its cerebral cortex. Maybe watching a bad film has the same halo effect that childbirth has on mothers. Just as, with childbirth, the effect and memory of the pain of parturition is overtaken by the feeling of reward and love for the child, so the memory of the pain from watching a film like *Hell Comes to Frogtown* (1987) is overtaken by the feeling of reward and love for simply being out of the cinema and into some fresh air.

The further away in time from the original viewing of a bad movie a person gets, the less they are able to remember of the plot and, most importantly, the more the memory fades of how bad it actually was. So, a day after the film, you will be able to remember snippets but not necessarily in order, and probably only certain images and the odd absurd line of dialogue. A year after the film and beyond, not only will you have just the vaguest memory of what it was about, you will have forgotten how awful it really was. You are daydreaming one day and suddenly a scene from *Glitter* (2001) comes back to you, and you remember thinking at the time how bad it was, but now you're not so sure. You find yourself thinking, 'It couldn't have been that bad. Nothing could be that bad. I seem to remember that Mariah Carey was quite good in it, actually. I think I enjoyed it. Yes, it was a good film.' This can be dangerous, as it leads a person to go back and re-watch the movie with a higher expectation, which can lead to nausea, vomiting and disorientation.

This misremembering is the only explanation I have come up with as to why I get so many angry e-mails from people when I dare to say a specific film is 'bad'. For example, we get a lot of flak for daring to show films like *Top Gun* (1986) and *Commando* (1985) as part of the Bad Film Club. Mainly because the men (and it is mostly men) who complain have memories of those movies tied up to their childhood. When their brain was still forming, the films' terribleness would have been lost in a haze of cider and masturbation, and misremembered as a happy, positive experience. We once had a gentleman walk out of the cinema when he found out we would be talking over the film *Basic Instinct 2*. Quite how we could have spoiled that movie by talking over it I don't know. I've tried to figure out what that man was so captivated by and why he was offended that we called it a bad movie. I mean, come on, I'm not even sure it qualifies as a movie. David Thewlis' Welsh accent alone is enough to categorise it as more of a living nightmare than an actual film.

If you follow the simple rules set out above, you will have as much fun as it is possible to have while watching a bad movie. Just remember to do what I say and not what I do. I am, after all, a professional bad-movie watcher, and much like a hunter of poisonous snakes, I have exposed myself over the years to the worst stories, acting and movie concepts available, which means I now have an extremely high tolerance. This guide will help you experience your bad movie safely, securely and with as little psychological and physical harm as possible. So now you're ready, which movie will you start with?

4
The Razzies

You can't really write a book about bad movies without mentioning the Golden Raspberry Awards, or the Razzies as they are better known. While the Hollywood elite don their most expensive jewels and designer gowns and parade up that well-worn red carpet, somewhere else another group of very different film-lovers are pulling on a pair of jeans and furiously dabbing a soup stain out of their favourite novelty T-shirt. And just as those elite are readying themselves for a ceremony of self-congratulation taking place in an opulent and lavish theatre lit by a thousand twinkling lights and just as many burning egos, around the corner, in a far less glamorous location, there is a room full of people who are just as eager to snuff those egos out. Each year, the Razzies, a raspberry in the face of Hollywood movies and their well-paid stars, recognise those who have caused audiences a degree of cinematic pain during the year. The organisers' mission statement is emblazoned on their website and makes it clear just exactly what they think of the Hollywood celebrity machine and its products:

> Tired of all those chi-chi showbiz awards shows that are wall-to-wall air kisses, back-slapping and brown-nosing? Wanna give All Those Over-the-Top AWFUL Celebrities a piece of your mind?? Then maybe you're ready to run with some BERRY BIG DOGS – the ones who BITE Hollywood's butt instead of kissing it! If you'd like to be a part of Tinsel Town's most amusing (and embarrassing) night, and have YOUR opinion be heard all over the world, HERE'S YOUR CHANCE!

It's almost as though these awards – which take the literal form of a small, gold-coloured raspberry on a plinth – are inspired by scrolling through *Variety* or looking at local cinema listings and becoming overwhelmed by the unoriginality and cold-hearted commercialism seemingly responsible for the overabundance of almost identical paint-by-numbers Hollywood mainstream movies. Not only are these movies derivative, but they also seem to be being produced and distributed within such close proximity to each other that the Razzie voters just can't help but make a comment. Because, really, that's what the Razzie is: a satirical comment on Hollywood and its pomposity. It's a bubble-popper, a cigarette butt in a glass of champagne; and unlike its more pretentious older brother, it never takes itself too seriously.

These awards are not so much a backlash against Hollywood, more a gentle slap-down back to reality; and they have been since the start of the 1980s. They were invented by John J B Wilson back in 1981 after he watched a double bill of now bad-movie classics, Robert Greenwald's *Xanadu* (1980) and Nancy Walker's Village People disco extravaganza *Can't Stop the Music* (1980). The first ceremony was held, although not in any official way, at a post-Academy Award party hosted by Wilson, who had asked his friends to give out these random awards in his living room. So, from a makeshift podium, it was announced that *Can't Stop the Music* had the honour of winning the very first Golden Raspberry award. And well deserved it was too. Anybody who has had to sit through Steve Guttenberg's roller-skating antics and Leatherman's rendition of Danny Boy (which draws people to him like they were wildlife enchanted by Snow White) would think the film deserves to win every year.

Other winners on that first night were Neil Diamond, who got the worst actor gong for his role in *The Jazz Singer* (1980), and Brooke Shields, who took the worst actress award for her performance in Randal Kleiser's *Blue Lagoon* (1980). There was a tie in the worst supporting actor category, between John Adams for his role as Phil Dawn in the John Cassavetes film

Gloria(1980) and Laurence Olivier, proving that actors with great reputations can find themselves tarred with the bad-movie brush, for his part as Cantor Rabinovitch in Richard Fleicher's *The Jazz Singer* (1980). Amy Irving was unfortunate to win the first award for worst supporting actress, for her contribution to Jerry Schatzberg's *Honeysuckle Rose* (1980) – but she managed to pull it back when she received an Academy Award nomination for her role in *Yentl* (1983) a few years later. As far as I'm concerned, the worst supporting actress award should have gone to Marilyn Sokol for playing Lulu in *Can't Stop the Music*, not only because of her terrible overacting but also because she acted like a marauding sex pest and looked like Tim Curry's Frankenfurter throughout the entire movie. I'm not sure if the costume designer was going for bag lady from the neck down and 'sweet transvestite' from the neck up, but that's what she got.

Luckily for *Xanadu*, it wasn't left coughing in the glitter dust trails of *Can't Stop the Music* for too long, as it picked up the first award for the worst director. But it lost out, again, to the Village People vehicle when Allan Carr won for worst screenplay.

Lastly, and most surprisingly, the winner of the worst original song on the night came from *neither* of the two musicals that were nominated; it actually came from Robert Day's comedy *The Man with Bogart's Face* (1980). The catchy song, also titled 'The Man with Bogart's Face', was written by George Duning and Andrew Fenady, and was a worthy winner. Although there can be no doubt that the acting, narrative and production values of *Xanadu* and *Can't Stop the Music* are genuinely the stuff of nightmares (I once dreamed I was one of the girls in the 'I Love You to Death' number from *Can't Stop the Music*, but I wasn't throwing red glitter, I was throwing scorpions and Lego heads, and I accidentally killed Rod Stewart – true story), but you can't really knock the songs; most of them are pretty good. I would encourage any of you who have not heard 'The Man with Bogart's Face' to search it out on YouTube so you too can enjoy the Casio keyboard demo funk setting, and hear blues guitar with added random trumpets playing alongside screeching session singers wailing out such classic lines as, 'See the man with Bogart's face, take your troubles to his place' and 'He's aces and got moxy, this dude is mightily foxy.' It's a long way from the genius of Joe Turano's song 'Everybody But You' from *Night Train to Terror* (1985), which repeats the line 'Dance with me, dance with me, dance with me, dance with me' until it's all you can think about for days afterwards, but it's clear to see why it bested the Village People's and Olivia Newton-John's efforts.

Since that first makeshift ceremony, the Razzie Awards have gained considerably in notoriety and popularity, especially with fans of terrible cinema, who look to them for confirmation of their movie stinkers, and with those who seek to deflate the pomp and ceremony of the Oscars and the bubble in which Hollywood can sometimes seal itself. What I find noteworthy about the Razzies is that although they do go after the worst movies of the year, they tend not to target smaller, independent, no-budget or straight-to-DVD films. Their aim has always been to highlight the cinematic crimes of the Hollywood mainstream. And that is something to be commended. It's easy to shoot bad-movie fish in a small barrel. It would be pointless to nominate *Sharknado* (2013) or *Snakes on a Plane* (2006) for worst picture, because they exist for the express reason of being a bad movie. It would be like Roger Ebert writing a scathing review of a badly-made, zero-budget, high-school-produced film that focuses on some social issue, but in a quirky way. Of course that film is going to be lit badly and sound as if the whole thing was shot inside a crisp packet. Yes, parts of it are going to be out of focus, and the tops of people's head are sometimes going to be off the screen because the camera operator doesn't know how to use a tripod properly and the director is more interested in updating his lunch status on Facebook.

No acclaimed actor is too big to be brought down a peg or two, and no renowned director is out of bounds, regardless of track record. Two-time Pulitzer Prize winner Norman Mailer tied for worst director in 1987 for his film *Tough Guys Don't Dance* (the other joint winner being Elaine May for *Ishtar*).

Multi-Academy Award nominee Dennis Hopper won worst supporting actor for his role as Deacon in Kevin Reynolds' *Waterworld* (1995). In some ways, the Razzies encapsulate all the things that bad movies, intentionally bad or not, stand for. A metaphorical middle finger to the egos of filmmakers and to the idea that there is only one way to make or enjoy a movie. The Academy Awards may be for the industry, but the Razzies are for the people who will not be told by Hollywood what films they ought to be watching.

Even the thinking behind the voting system is wildly different. If you want to become a member of the voting panel for the Academy Awards, you need to be working in the film industry and be able to demonstrate a back catalogue of consistent and quality productions. As well as the quality, you have to have the quantity; so, writers have to have at least two screenplay credits and actors at least three credited film roles, and the tech lot (you know, the ones who actually make the film possible but are usually rushed through during the ceremonies or not even televised because they are ordinary-looking) must be active in the industry, or have been so for a number of years. This means that it's possible to get on the Academy Awards panel even if you're not particularly good at your job; you just need a couple of credits and a buddy who is already on the panel to give you a glowing reference. Paul W S Anderson – *Mortal Kombat* (1995), *Death Race* (2008) – has more than two credits and a body of work, but do you really want him deciding what constitutes a 'good' movie? Once your application is in, members of the board will look you over and decide whether or not you are the sort of person they want judging the work of others. By contrast, if you would like to be a part of the Golden Raspberry Awards judging panel, all you need is a PayPal account and $40. There certainly don't seem to be any vetting processes, no letter of reference, no need to prove a body of work, a job or even an interest in the film industry. It isn't even specified that members actually have to *see* the movies. No waiting list, no approval waiting time and no industry experience necessary; all you need is a functioning hand (or surrogate hand) to make your vote and, of course, $40.

The Razzie organisers have in fact been criticised for the ease with which they allow their members to join and vote, but I feel that criticism is unfair. If you are an actor sitting on the Academy Awards panel, you're going to be looking at the performance from a professional actor's point of view; you're going to understand the pressures, the time constraints, the processes of character development and all the rest of the pre-performance stuff that actors claim to put themselves through before shooting a film. But Dave the trainee plumber, who has paid upwards of nine quid for a cinema ticket and taken out a second mortgage to buy a large drink and some popcorn, isn't going to care about the processes or the preparation. He's going to be sat in his sticky seat amongst the discarded sweet wrappers, with popcorn all down his shirt – because it's impossible to eat popcorn any other way – sipping on a soda the size of a Fiat Cinquecento, expecting the actors to say the lines that have been written for them and hoping for it not to suck.

Those not affiliated with the film industry are also going to be influenced by the quality of the rest of the movie when they come to make their individual category votes. Very rarely will you hear somebody say something like, 'I saw that movie *Jack and Jill* today. It was such a terrible film, I mean really bad, it made me want to scratch my eyes out and stick knitting needles in my ears. But, saying that, you have to hand it to Katie Holmes, she did a sterling job considering the circumstances. Imagine the pressures she must have been subjected to.' If the movie was crap then the acting was crap, and if the acting was crap then the director was crap and the soundtrack was crap and everybody who worked on the project was crap. As audience members, we should have the right to express that even more so than those who work in the industry, because we are the ones paying for the tickets.

The Razzies, every now and then, also like to throw in an extra award prompted by and representing a swell of opinion from audiences and organisers alike, taking their cue from the films that have been nominated that year. For example, the 1997 awards included a gong for Worst Reckless Disregard for Human Life and Public Property, the winner of which was director Simon West's over-the-top action extravaganza *Con Air*. This Nicholas Cage-starring classic managed to beat dinosaur epic *The Lost World: Jurassic Park*, the 'not as good as *Turbulence 3* (2001), which was a hilariously bad movie' *Turbulence*, the Tommy Lee Jones and Anne Heche film *Volcano* and the super camp and super dull *Batman and Robin*. I think the organisers should have created a special award just for *Batman and Robin*, for 'Greatest Number of Nonsensical Puns Uttered in Two Hours of My Life that I Will Never Get Back'. Other specially-created awards have included 2003's Worst Excuse for an Actual Movie, won by *The Cat in the Hat*, and 2010's Worst Eye-Gouging Misuse of 3D – a technology that passes in and out of cinematic fashion – which surprisingly didn't go *to Cats and Dogs 2: Revenge of Kitty Galore* but was won by *The Last Airbender*.

So far, my all-time-favourite special award title was created in 2002 for Most Flatulent Teen-Targeted Movie – a response, perhaps, to the number of money-driven, specific-demographic-targeted movies that came out that year. With stiff competition from Seth Kearsley's *Eight Crazy Nights*, Tamra Davis's Britney Spears vehicle *Crossroads*, Raja Gosnell's annoying CGI dog house movie *Scooby-Doo*, and migraine-inducing Vin Diesel action movie *XXX* from producer Rob Cohen, the award was won by the team behind *Jackass: The Movie*. Hard to believe that in 2002 there existed only one *Jackass* movie. I envy you people of 2002, I really do.

As well as the special categories, the Razzie organisers will sometimes slip in more, for want of a better word, abstruse nominations into their normal categories. In 2006, one of the nominations for Worst Screen Couple was 'Sharon Stone's lopsided breasts' in *Basic Instinct 2*; and in 2014, when the awards celebrated their thirty-fifth year, the Worst Screen Combo category had a nomination for 'Any two robots' from *Transformers: Age of Extinction* and was won by Kirk Cameron and his ego for *Saving Christmas*.

In 2015, not only did the organisers of the Razzies ceremony open its doors to the public for the first time, meaning that fellow fans of bad movies could be part of the fun, they also included a new category. Rather than a one-off special category, this one looks as though it is here to stay; and the thinking behind it, once again, highlights the true sporting nature of the awards. The new category is the Razzie Redeemer Award, and its primary function is 'acknowledging those who've gone from being Razzie targets to doing far, far better things'. This seems to signify the Razzies taking a small step into a more mature attitude toward the films they nominate, and showing that they are self-effacing enough to stand next to the people who have won a Razzie in the past and congratulate them on their improvements and achievements.

Amongst the nominees for the inaugural Razzie Redeemer Award were Ben Affleck, Mike Myers and Kristen Stewart. Affleck won his original Razzie award for a trifecta of bad movies, *Gigli* (2003), *Daredevil* (2003) and *Paycheck* (2003). His nomination in the new category acknowledged his strength and fortitude in managing to climb out of his Jay-Lo quagmire and into such films as *Argo* (2012) and *Gone Girl* (2014). Myers was nominated for going from the painfully unfunny *Love Guru* (2008) to legitimate documentary director of *Supermensch: The Legend of Shep Gordon* (2013). Carved-wooden-statue-who-has-almost-come-to-life Kristen Stewart, who won her Razzie for sulking her way through *Twilight* (2008), qualified for redeemable status thanks to her far better performance in *Still Alice* (2014). Proving that they can give credit where credit is due, and in the spirit of forgiveness, the organisers arranged for world-renowned film critic and wife of God, Sister Rose Pacatte, to give out the award. There could be only one winner, and that was Ben Affleck. Anybody who can pull themselves out of that big of a career slump deserves a prize. However, I'm waiting to see his performance as Batman before I pass judgement on whether or not he really has turned his long history of losing streaks into a winning one.

When I first heard of the new Razzie Redeemer Award, I wondered if it might be something the panel of the Academy Awards would be willing to try out, but in reverse. Let's be honest, there are *far* more actors who go from Academy Award winners to appearing in straight-to-DVD clunkers or working at a TGI Fridays, or in soft-core porn. It can happen to the best of them. Just look at Jon Voight, who went from *Coming Home* (1979), which won him a Best Actor Oscar, to starring in *Anaconda* (1997), for which he received Razzie nominations for Worst Actor and Worst Screen Couple. Not to mention multi-Academy Award nominee and winner Al Pacino, who picked up a golden statue for *Scent of a Woman* (1992) and then slid from acting demigod to acting like a pillock in films such as *Gigli* and *Jack and Jill* (2011). Surely there should be a segment of the Academy Awards in which all of the actors who have made a mockery of their previous Oscar nominations and wins – I'm looking at you, Nicolas Cage – have to get up on stage and hand their award back to the panel?

There are some in Hollywood who 'get' the Razzies and are happy to hold up their hands and admit to putting out a box office turkey from time to time; and there have been a few instances where, to their credit, those nominated have graciously accepted their awards in the spirit in which they are intended, and even in person. Probably the two most famous in-person recipients of a Razzie have been Halle Berry and Sandra Bullock. Berry was nominated in the Worst Actress category for *Catwoman* (2004), and what a well-deserving win it was. That movie was one of the worst I've ever sat through. I just didn't understand why she turned into a cat. I still don't know why she turned into a cat, and if you think I'm going to sit through that movie again to figure it out, you've got another think coming. I'd rather get cat AIDS than sit through that movie again. The Bad Film Club were once booked to do a live commentary over *Catwoman* in a Durham arts centre, but when we turned up, they didn't have any microphones; apparently the guys who booked the show didn't mention that we might be needing them to perform a live commentary. One of the ushers said we could use the public address system, until I pointed out that it would mean the entire building being subjected to our commentary. Susan on the concession stand doesn't need to hear us two swearing at Halle Berry as she's dishing out popcorn. There was much chatter and brainstorming but, by this time, people had started to file in to the cinema, and we were frantically scrambling about still trying to find a microphone alternative. Eventually it became clear that this wasn't going to happen, so we skulked back to the screening room to inform the audience of the mix-up. As soon as we opened the doors at the back of the cinema screen, we heard the music and the lights went off. They had started the film without us. To our shame, we just hightailed it out of there. So, to the people of Durham who had to sit through *Catwoman* with no help or support from us whatsoever, we apologise profusely. It must have been very traumatic for you. But we were cowards who saw an opportunity not to have to watch that terrible film again, and we took it. *And we would do it again!*

In fairness to her, Halle Berry's speech at the Razzie ceremony was a wonderful tongue-in-cheek parody of the Oscar speech she gave after winning the Best Actress award for *Monster's Ball* in 2002. She walked onto the stage to similar rapturous applause, doing her very best crying acting, while carrying her Academy Award in one hand and her Razzie in the other. Fake crying aside, she then gave her official speech, which started off with, 'Thank you, guys. I never in my life thought I would be up here ... I have so many people to thank, because you don't win a Razzie without a lot of help from a lot of people.' The fact that her speech was peppered with screams of 'I love you' and frequent whoops of excitement from the audience demonstrates that the awards are not really given or meant to be taken in malice. The audience weren't baying for Berry's blood, they were happy to see her, and even happier to know that she 'got' it. She even brought out onto the stage a weeping Alex Brostein, one of her co-stars on the movie and better known as the voice of Lois in *Family Guy*, whom she thanked for lying to her face every day about the quality of her performance. She ended by saying how she would take the criticism on board, but that she hoped to god that she would never see any of the Razzie panel again.

Sandra Bullock was at the ceremony a few years later to pick up two awards for her involvement in Phil Traill's movie *All About Steve* (2009), for which she was nominated for Worst Actress and, for her lack of on-screen chemistry with co-star Bradley Cooper, Worst Screen Couple. If you've never seen it, *All About Steve* is supposedly a romantic comedy, but I would dispute that, as it is about an obsessive woman stalking a man whom she believes to be her true love. It's a confused mess of a film that is too mainstream to be a quirky indie and too inconsistent to be a real mainstream Hollywood rom-com. The most annoying thing is that Bullock's character, Mary Magdalene Horowitz (sigh), can't make up her mind whether she's a sassy-talking smartarse or a dizzy blonde airhead. She changes her character to suit each scene, and does whatever is needed to help chug the plot along.

Bullock's acceptance speech had a little bit more attitude than Halle Berry's; she strolled onto the stage with a little red cart full of *About Steve* DVDs to distribute to the audience members. She also brought out a script, which she opened in readiness to dissect the narrative as she cracked jokes about the box office figures: 'They said nobody went to go see this film, but I know there's over 700 members here, and if I won, that means the majority of the 700 had to have voted, so that means 352 [watched it].' Again, when Bullock came onto the stage with her free DVDs, the audience cheered; they didn't boo her or refuse the films. They called and yelled excitedly, like an Oprah audience who have just been told to look under their seats. Bullock also made a deal with the panel: she said that if they agreed to watch the film again, and decided to rethink their decision to award the movie two Razzies, she would come back the following year and give back the award. She did eventually give the Razzie back, but only because she had mistakenly taken the original prototype instead of one of the cheap ones they actually give out at the ceremony. The ceremonial awards cost $4.79 each; that original prototype, in nostalgia terms, is priceless. There have been a few non-actors who have also collected their awards in person. They are of no lesser importance than the actors – we're not at the Academy Awards now, after all. Writer J D Shapiro was awarded the Razzie twice for the same movie, *Battlefield Earth* (2000), the Scientology-inspired science fiction flick starring John Travolta. At a Bad Film Club screening of that long and arduous movie at the Barbican Centre in London, about twenty members of Anonymous – the hacktivist and anti-Scientologist protest group – came along to see the move, and they all sat in the same row with their *V for Vendetta* masks on. There was certainly a tension in the audience, and during the pre-film talk, one of them stood up and yelled, 'We are Anonymous', to which my buddy and Bad Film Club co-founder Joe replied, 'Dave? Is that you?' A few laughs of relief popped the hostility as the audience realised the Anonymous members were no threat and the masked massive realised we were no Scientologists, and we all realised that *Battlefield Earth* deserves to be dropped into a live volcano along with a few hydrogen bombs.

Shapiro accepted the award for *Battlefield Earth*, the first time, from founder John Wilson, but this wasn't at the official ceremony, it was during the broadcast of a weekend talk radio show called *Drastic Radio with Mark Ebner*. It was during this talk with Ebner about making the movie that Shapiro revealed that John Travolta had read the first draft of the script and called it 'The *Schindler's List* of science fiction' – which, when you see it written down like that, makes perfect sense and is in no way the stupid-fucking-est thing you'll read today. When you compare them side by side, it's obvious what he was talking about. One is a film about a man who is concerned about the constant persecution of his Jewish workforce by members of the Nazi party, who are brutally oppressing all as they see fit. The other is about John Travolta and Forest Whitaker prancing about in leather pants sporting matted dreadlock hairstyles usually found on the heads of blonde middle-class kids off to somewhere in Asia on a gap year. Shapiro later made an in-person appearance at the ceremony to accept the special anniversary Razzie for Worst Picture of the Decade in 2010, where he quoted a line he credited to the *New York Times*, '*Battlefield Earth* is about the extinction of the human race, and after seeing this movie, I'm all for it' – which is how most of us felt after the ordeal of watching it.

One of the few people to have ungraciously accepted a Razzie in person is comedian and actor Bill Cosby – although winning a Razzie is probably the least awkward topic to bring up from his past. It sure seems like a quick journey from 'grandfather' of comedy to 'dodgy man in the corner whom you wouldn't want to buy you a drink' of comedy. Cosby was actually the first actor to accept a Razzie personally. This was for the Paul Weiland film *Leonard Part 6* (1987) early on in 1988, when the awards were still in their makeshift stages. The film was actually nominated for five awards: Worst Picture, Worst Actor, Worst Screenplay, Worst Supporting Actress (Gloria Foster) and Worst Director. Of these, Cosby himself won two, Worst Actor and Worst Screenplay. Apparently, upon hearing of his 'victory', Cosby made a point of saying that he wanted to receive his award, and if it wasn't golden he was going to go to the press. This discourteous attitude rattled the Razzie panel because, perhaps for the first time since the awards were invented, a member of the Hollywood pack was taking them seriously.

An actual award was cobbled together, which was intended to be presented to Cosby during a late-night segment on the Fox network. However, perhaps to put down the Razzie organisers, Fox had other plans, and handed Cosby their own version of the award, fashioned from 24-carat gold and marble and costing approximately $30,000! An action I still find annoying some 28 years later, because, to me, Fox creating that valuable statue actually devalued the award. The Razzie represents shonky work – be that shonky acting, screenwriting or any other of the components needed to create a film – and the award *needs* to reflect that. The Academy Award statue is made of sleek gold-plated alloy, the BAFTA is made of bronze; both are representative of the high esteem in which the winners are held by the panel of judges. On the other hand, the Teen Choice award is a surfboard, and the Nickelodeon trophy and the British Comedy Award trophy are both made of plastic. It stands to reason that the less weighty the award, the less money it should take to make it. As mentioned earlier, the Razzie costs a mere $4.97 to make, and that is how it should be. Handing Bill Cosby a $30,000 statue is equivalent to presenting an Academy Award made from Diet Coke cans and bits of old chewing gum. It's insulting, and totally missing the point of what the statue represents. The connotative meaning behind that tiny golden raspberry should be, 'We thought your film was garbage; here, have this small, cheap and ugly trinket to remind you never to make a film this bad again.'

I will continue to love the Razzies and their ongoing work to make Hollywood studios aware of their mistakes; be they box-office flops or films that are goldmines for money but cesspits for quality – *cough* Michael Bay *cough*. They are the awards Hollywood should be turning to and using as a yardstick for gauging audience tastes and tolerances, looking at trends in the types of film that people don't want rather than second-guessing what they do. The awarding of the Razzies remains an important date in any bad-movie-lover's diary, and they are growing in popularity every year; but part of me hopes that they don't become too popular, as I would hate for them to get caught up in the glamour of Hollywood.

5
Lessons Learned: What Bad Movies Have Taught Me

As well as being entertaining and, at times, spirit-crushingly awful, watching a disproportionate amount of bad movies over the past twenty years has taught me many things.

Pearls of wisdom drip from the badly-conceived narrative and cinematography like drops of effervescent snot that others may discard into a tissue but I treasure and examine. That is not to say that everyday 'normal' movies don't offer sage advice; they most certainly do. But because the audience watching them are so enraptured and absorbed in the narrative that they actually care about the characters, the more subtle aspects of the film can pass them by. Luckily for us, the lovers of terrible movies, we are so alienated by the absurdity of the movies in front of us that we can take the time to decode their messages, and also to point out all of their continuity errors.

But not all bad-film fans have watched as many terrible films as many times as I have. I've never met another person who has sat through the whole of the Nu Image film *Octopus* (2000) once, let alone eight times. By choice. So in this chapter I've helpfully broken down the lessons I've learned from watching these bad movies for you, so that you don't have watch them yourself.

Expect the unexpected

It seems churlish and nonsensical to instruct a person to expect the unexpected. On the face of it, that makes no sense. How can a person ever expect what cannot be expected? I live my life expectantly waiting for the unexpected arrival of John Cusack to make me pancakes for breakfast. So far, nothing, but I live in hope. What I mean is that, in film terms, you should never take for granted that a bad film is going to play by the rules of conventional filmmaking, narrative or common sense. You have to unlearn all that you have subconsciously learned about how movies are constructed and what the expectations are, and be prepared to accepted whatever bat-shit crazy twists and turns are thrown at you.

There have been many bad movies that have shocked me, but one that honestly took me by surprise was a blaxploitation movie called *Soul Vengeance* (1975), aka *Welcome Home Brother Charles*. It's fair to say that blaxploitation movies have a reputation for being ostentatious and poorly conceived, but this one is in a league of its own. Small-time drug dealer Charles Murray, played by Marlo Monte (an actor who vanishes from cinematic history after this, his first and only credited movie role), finds himself embroiled in a police takedown where a violently racist cop arrests him and then beats him up in the back of the police van. The racist cop doesn't hold back in this movie, although at one point the other cops step in to *try* to hold him back from attempting to take out every black character he meets. During the needless beating in the van by PC Racist Hillbilly Badcop III (that's the name I have given him), Charles gets stabbed in his gentleman's how-do-you-do. Men are naturally very fond of their little soldiers, so obviously you would imagine that this attack is going to scar Charles both physically and mentally; but in fact it's never mentioned again. Not once. Charles is sent to jail, probably for the crime of being black and in possession of a bleeding man tube (it really was a different time back then), but if you're expecting to see the rough and tumble of black prison life you'll be disappointed. What the film actually does is show a series of black-and-white pictures of Charles in jail looking rather glum and pulling poses like he's in a depressing Calvin Klein underpants commercial.

When he comes out of jail, our Charles vows vengeance on those who put him behind bars, and in particular on the one who stabbed him in his private trouser sausage. And so he starts a profound shagging and killing spree. But there's something in this movie that doesn't seem right. Women appear to be hypnotised by Charles, as demonstrated in the scene where he seduces the wife of one of his victims in an up-against-the-wall sex-having act that even Elizabeth Hurley would say needed a bit of work. I'm sure the actress was going for 'I'm under a spell', but what she delivered was 'I wonder if there are chips in the freezer for dinner tonight.'

While Charles is busying himself with his killing and his seeking revenge, we only really see his face juxtaposed with the screams of his victims. Which is puzzling. It's not made clear how he is killing them. Is he stabbing them in *their* gentleman's sausage? Is he shooting them? Is he strangling them? It's a guessing game that isn't solved until about 12 minutes from the end, when all is revealed. Literally. As Charles corners his latest victim on the bed – a victim, by the way, who kind of deserves to be murdered for the crime of wearing a short silk kimono and white socks – it starts to becomes crystal clear how he has been murdering and hypnotising his prey. As his victim writhes around on the bed in pain, the bad quality of the film stock makes it difficult at first to understand what you are seeing. Is that a shadow or a snake or a rope? What is that thing crawling toward the guy? It is then you are rewarded with a clear close-up of the victim being strangled by something, and the triumphant emergence of the unmistakable bell-end of a black penis slapping up against the man's cheek. It would appear that Charles has been commanding his penis to grow up to seven or eight feet in length and then using it to vengefully crush his victims to death, like a well-trained trouser anaconda. Nobody can say that they expected that. Nobody. Especially when there has been no prior hint of it at all during the film.

Perhaps if there had been some kind of plastic-surgery scene, some form of bionic dong operation where a secret government military experiment was carried out to mutate cocks into finely-tuned killing machines – 'We can make it faster, stronger, longer, more killy around the tip' – then fair enough, I could *almost* accept it. But just to throw in, right at the end of the movie, the fact that the main protagonist has a magic murdering schlong, really does do justice to the phrase, 'That's not what I was expecting.' This has also managed to muddy my expectations of other movies; each time I see one where the murder weapon isn't revealed straight away, my mind instantly goes to the slaughtering schmekel.

The unexpected doesn't always have to be a man with a magic killing penis. Sometimes it can just be how a character looks or acts. You'd assume the most surprising part of the Village People's musical *Can't Stop the Music* (1980) would be how the myriad of gay sex references got past the censors, or the full-frontal male nakedness in the background of the 'YMCA' song changing-room scene, or the sequence of a midget buying yams at the Erotic Bakery (all of which are in the movie). But it's actually the wardrobe choice of the character played by ex-track and field athlete and ex-Kardashian dad Bruce Jenner that provides the movie's biggest shock. Previously portrayed as a stuffy lawyer in a three-piece suit, once he gets in with the in crowd, he frees himself from the constricting cloth and appears on screen walking down a New York street wearing blue denim short shorts (and I mean short shorts; Brother Charles certainly would not have been able to keep his secret if he'd been wearing these bad boys) and a woman's crop top. The short shorts I can kind of forgive; the 1970s were coming to an end and nobody was sure what the acceptable length of leg wear in the following decade would be. In fairness, Steve Guttenberg's aspiring singer character is also sporting some short tight whites. But the choice of the ladies' crop top is a curious one. It certainly wasn't chosen to show off Jenner's abs; but what it does do is draw the viewer's eyes downwards, via his rather hairy 'snail trail', to the denim-clad pouch beneath. Who would have thought that out of a group of guys that includes the Village People, Bruce Jenner would turn out to look the most flamboyant? Of course, hindsight is 20/20, and the transformation of Bruce Jenner into

Caitlyn Jenner goes some way to explaining why Bruce didn't mind getting out of the stuffy suit and into something a little more freeing. The world may have been rocked by the emergence of Caitlyn Jenner in 2015, but we bad film fans already witnessed the start of the change back in 1980.

Things that pass for 'terrifying creatures' can also catch you off guard, especially when you compare the promising DVD cover art with what you actually get to see in the film. Take *Boggy Creek II: And the Legend Continues* (1985) and *Snowbeast* (1977) as examples. The cover of *Boggy Creek II* features a howling creature, a terrifying image of a monster that will haunt your nightmares and rip your throat out as soon as look at you. In the film itself, however, the actual monster appears to be nothing more than a man in an ill-fitting gorilla suit. He's all baggy around the neck and the arms, and his face-mask keeps slipping past his eye make-up. Luckily for our adventurer Dr Lockheart, played by Charles B Pierce, another character who dons the denim short shorts to surprise the audience, it's not a horrible monster, it's just a mother monster who wants her baby back from the creepy hillbilly who has been keeping it hostage. It's probably best that we gloss over what a lonely man in the woods might want with a small ape chained up in the spare bedroom.

A similar type of gorilla suit can be found clad around the poor actor who plays *Snowbeast*'s Yeti monster, but this one is painted white and given a slightly more melted face. The most shocking and unexpected part of *Snowbeast*, though, is that we get to see the monster at all. It takes a while, with the director adopting the *Jaws* approach and filming most of the Yeti attacks as point-of-view shots that fade to red. Then, when we finally *do* get to see it, the Yeti goes all out and disrupts the preparations for the crowning of a high school carnival queen. Which is a shame, because they've gone to the bother of decorating the school gym with upwards of eight balloons and have thirty glasses of orange squash ready for the revellers. If that wasn't heinous enough, the Yeti then strolls into the car-park and punches a lesbian through a car window.

Regardless of where they are, actors are gonna act

If the most infamous incident in *Teen Wolf* (1985) – the one where a supporting artist supposedly gets his chappie out of his trousers in the bleachers at the basketball court in the final scene – has taught us anything, it's that no matter if the actors are in the foreground or the background, they are always going to be acting. Background actors are an integral part of almost every movie's make-up. Without them, there would be no crowd scenes, no café ambience and no awkward dancing-in-a-nightclub-to-different-beats scenes. In big productions, there are crew members whose job it is to keep an eye on the background actors to make sure there's no mugging or looking into the camera and that they're blending into the background and supporting the main protagonists. However, even the 'extras wrangler', director and editor with the keenest eyes still managed to miss that shot of a Stormtrooper bumping his head that made it into the final cut of Star Wars.

The movies that I love, the ones made by directors who couldn't tell you what time it is, let alone what is happening in front of the camera, are unsurprisingly a little more lax. This lack of attention to detail gives the 'supporting artists' a chance to show off their acting prowess. As I always say, just because they're in the background doesn't mean they're not acting their little hearts out; after all, they want their friends and family to notice them when they see the movie.

Once you become aware of one background artist pulling focus in a film it becomes distracting and can change your film-watching experience. Find one and you start looking for more; and the more you find, the less attention you pay to the foreground, until you're half-way through the movie and have no idea what it is about. Bad films have taught me that, most of the time, the background is more entertaining than the foreground. And you can afford to enjoy it, because bad movies don't require a lot of your attention. For example, you wouldn't think that anything could out-act Debbie Gibson and a half-masticated whale rotting on a beach, but in *Mega Shark vs. Giant*

Octopus (2009) the three extras employed to play security guys make an excellent job of it. Hats off to them, they've come dressed in full men-in-black regalia, complete with aviator shades and communication devices, and it's obvious that they are determined to mug their way through every shot they are in. They stand behind the main actors and talk sternly into their communicators, they march around with purpose, crossing and uncrossing their arms, looking over their shades and pushing them back up again as they keep an eye on the action, ready to act fast in case of an intruder. At one point, the extra in the middle starts talking to the two behind him. He over-gesticulates with every sentence, then starts pointing at the dead whale as the others shrug as if to say that, no, they have no idea what is going on either. It's like a short play the three of them have rehearsed beforehand. I can imagine them sat in a car at the beach car-park running through their bit: 'Roy, you and I will be playing these, like, really tough secret service agent guys, and Steve, you'll be, like, the new guy, and you'll be, like, all excited at this strange turn of events and we'll be, like, "Calm down kid, you see a lot of crazy ass shit in this business. Get used to it."' As Gibson is having an argument with her boss about borrowing a super-high-tech submarine and not telling anybody she took it, one of the security extras manages to get his head right in between those of the two actors and spends their conversation nodding along with the aggrieved scientist and shaking his head judgementally at Gibson. It's clear whose side this guy is on: his character is working for the Man.

There are many times in moviemaking when you need to film a crowd scene, but there are also times when you can't afford a crowd. It's all very well if you're Richard Attenborough or William Wyler, but a modest budget won't stretch to 10,000-plus extras, even at a pay rate of crisps and unlimited public bathroom tap water, so bad-film makers have to keep their shots tight to make it look like the eight people who turned up are actually a bloodthirsty baying mob. In *Turbulence 3: Heavy Metal* (2001), Marilyn Manson lookalike Slade Craven (played by John Mann) and his band of Gothic punk hell-raisers arrive at an airport in readiness for their online streaming gig, which is to take place on a plane. (Talk about sticking it to the Man. Nobody would expect these guys to do a gig on a plane; they're probably going to sneak an extra meal and tell the cabin staff to fuck off when asked to put up their tray tables and return their chairs to the upright position. They are crazy cats.) As Craven walks up to the airport entrance, his path is lined either side with pro-Craven and anti-Craven protesters; the pro contingent on one side with their black make-up and ripped trousers, the anti on the other with their sensible cardigans and tight perms. Neither side seems particularly dedicated to the cause until a television reporter does a piece to camera with the rampant pro-Craven team behind him. Being directly behind a protagonist is, for some extras, the next best thing to getting themselves an actual speaking part, so for a small gaggle to be told to 'act angry' while looking into the camera, it must have been a dream come true. It appears, however, that most of these extras had never even heard a metal song; and, as supporting artists, maybe they just didn't have the acting chops to be able to comprehend the way that fans of Gothic / metal / punk / shoutyshouty music would behave. They can be seen bouncing behind the reporter, manifestly tired from having to flash the rock hand gesture all day, with one or two of them looking far too old to be wearing far too little. Not that there should be an age limit to a genre of music, but if your clothes say, 'I'm a cyberpunk fucker,' but your face says, 'I'd rather be having a cup of tea,' the sincerity of your rock hand gestures is going to be brought into question.

The pro-Craven team are also brandishing homemade banners, which all contain similar messages daubed on similar cards – amazing slogans such as 'I ♥ Slade' and 'Do me Craven.' It's sad that the invention of Tinder and Grindr has all but done away with a person's ability to find a rock-star boyfriend or girlfriend by writing how much you'd like to have sex with them on a bit of cardboard and waving it about in public. Technology, it will kill us all.

Making the evil punk-ass pro-Craven team even less

credible is a man whose arm is seen way at the back of the crowd, wearing a lovely, comfy red jumper. Maybe he was originally part of the anti-Craven team and was swayed over by the compelling argument of the black-lipstick-wearing woman who just stands there and gives the middle finger. 'You make a good point, madam, I shall join your side.' There is also, standing right behind the reporter, a woman who doesn't seem to know what she is supposed to be chanting, and so just makes a kind of *mamamama* motion with her lips. She's still acting, though. She may not understand *what* she's acting, but she's going for it – that is, in between the nine or twelve times she stops what she's doing to make sure her hat is still at a jaunty angle. You have to get these things right; what if a major Hollywood director needed a character who wore a hat for his/her next movie? She has to prove that she can wear it well.

On the other, anti-Craven side, the supporting artists fare little better as the slick news reporter swings around to give them their camera time. Their placards are white, whereas the other side's are black; it's as if they're *trying* to be different. The director doesn't seem to have taken much notice of these boards either, as they suggest a clash of ideologies. Amongst those that read 'Say NO to violence' and 'What happened to Humanity?' there are others displaying messages such as 'Burn in Hell' and the word 'Metal' followed by the Nazi swastika. (I don't know why I felt the need to write *Nazi* swastika there; I can't imagine many of you would have been thinking, 'What, the Hindu sign for good fortune?') I can't help but feel that those on the anti-Craven team have got into it a little more than those on the pro-Craven team. They are yelling, shaking their heads and pulling their most angry faces. These extras are really acting their socks off! The camera flips back and forth between middle-finger-brandishing pros and crucifix-brandishing antis, and most of them look uncomfortable to be there. Perhaps they should all have been placed in the middle with banners that read, 'I don't know what I'm doing, but I'm still an actor and I'm in a film.'

Sometimes it's not that the extras are overacting, it's that what they are doing is too damned distracting. In *Who Dares*

Wins (1982), our hero and tiptop-tough guy Peter Skellen, played by Lewis Collins from *The Professionals*, is having a super-secret rendezvous with his super-secret boss in a super-clandestine meeting spot in an underground car-park. It looks as though only two types of people use the car-park: undercover police wanting privacy from the public and roller-skating gymnasts. The trouble is, when you have those two groups together in a scene, no matter how much tension the director wants to create, nothing is going to bring a thrilling meeting to a juddering halt like the sight of a roller-skating woman in leg warmers gliding about on one leg in the background. It's just too distracting. Imagine the most intimate and important conversation you've ever had with a person. Now imagine having that conversation with a group of body-popping break-dancers next to you and tell me if its gravitas is still intact. What doesn't help matters is that the scene in question in back-lit, which makes the skater even more obvious as she glides by, doing tricks and super-cool manoeuvres in shiny leggings. The consequence being that, every time I see that scene, my brain won't stop singing the Cliff Richard song 'Wired for Sound'.

All's well that just ends

If there are any screenwriters or students of cinema reading this then you might already be familiar with certain narrative theories. Todorov's theory that all narrative has a sequence of events from equilibrate disequilibrium to new equilibration; the three-act structure; the classic linear narrative; Barthes' five codes; etc. Others may be unaware of any of these but still instinctively know from years of film-watching that there are certain things expected of a movie; and an ending is certainly one of them. What bad movies have taught me, however, is that if a script arrives with no ending, it doesn't necessarily mean it won't get made. Sometimes it's okay if a bad film just ends, or if it has an ending that opens up more questions than it answers: the truth is, the audience are just happy to be leaving the cinema.

I'll again use one of my all-time favourite bad movies, *Jaws The Revenge* (1987), as a prime example of how little respect Hollywood, or just left of Hollywood, can sometimes have for its movies, its narratives and its audiences. I've already explained how this movie's ending was changed because the original was considered either too rubbish or too gruesome, depending on who you ask. Nobody liked the original version of the final death scene – which saw the boat ramming into the grudge-bearing shark while it was doing a wheelie on its tail (no, they can't really do that), resulting in its head being speared off and both shark and boat breaking apart – and the re-edited replacement was scarcely better. It's not that final death scene I take issue with, though; I made my peace with it a long time ago. My problem is with the movie's actual concluding scene, once the shark has been vanquished and the Brody family are back in their rough-edged shack of a house, happy and finally at peace.

Ellen has decided that she's going to pootle off home and is hitching a ride with Hoagie on his private plane. Once again she is getting away from all things that remind her of shark attacks, going back to Amity Island where there are only happy memories of shark-induced child murder, the death of her son and the death of her husband to help her sleep at night. What bothers me is that the family are all joking and smiling and happily bidding farewell to each other, and at no point does anybody say, 'Dude, do you remember the other day when we totally blew up that giant shark,' or, 'Hey, Ellen, you know your son who you buried about ten days ago? Are you over him now, or what?' There is none of that; the film just ends. Ellen says goodbye, gets on the plane and the credits roll. No explanation, no hint of getting counselling sessions to recover from what they've been through; nobody has learned anything and nobody has changed. I suppose the lack of explanation is a cinematic '... and they all lived happily ever after, now go to sleep and no you can't have another drink of water and don't bother me, mummy is drinking her special drink watching her Ryan Reynolds movie.' The audience may crave closure, but all they get is credits. What of the relationship between Michael and Ellen? The relationship between Michael and Jake? The relationship between Jake and the sea snails? Didn't the giant shark garner any kind of press coverage? And what measures have been taken to ensure that another shark isn't going to swim in with the same murderous intentions? The kind of disrespect the entire narrative is given by the ending means the last scene could just as well be a floating middle finger, or a flashing sign that says, 'It all meant nothing.' And it's the most common ending to many a bad movie. It's as if nobody actually cares about the conclusion, just as long as the middle bit has tits and gore in it.

An unsatisfactory and strange kind of ending *Jaws The Revenge* might have, but at least it does have some conclusion with the destruction of the shark. Unlike the overly colourful, incomprehensible crap-fest that is Chris Sivertson's *I Know Who Killed Me* (2007). This film isn't one of Lindsay Lohan's finest moments; and when you look at her post-puberty filmography, that's a damning statement. Its relentless blue and red iconography – presumably from the mind of cinematographer John R Leonetti, who also worked on such visual greats as *Child's Play 3* (1991) and *Mortal Combat* (1995) – is like being bashed over the head repeatedly with the most basic of metaphors. Blue is cold, red is hot, they are opposites, the characters are opposites, one is a calm and studious girl and the other is a pole-dancing stripper. They. Are. Different. There is a lot more blue than any other colour; blue filters, blue glass, blue veils; the entire film looks like it's been ejaculated on by a Smurf.

Some time after Aubrey Fleming (Lohan) has been reported missing, she is found by a passing car, covered in blood and with parts of her body missing. She is taken to hospital, where she wakes up with half a leg and half an arm to see a relieved family she doesn't remember, who take her home to a house she says she has never seen before. Although everybody around her is calling her Aubrey Fleming, she is insisting her name is actually Dakota Moss. Clearly she is suffering from post-traumatic stress from the attack – and the fact that she has been given an overly-large bionic hand to replace the one that 'fell off' probably isn't helping. Maybe there was a hospital administration error and she was given the prosthetic hand of a 45-year-old plumber. After what seems like hours of wankily-filmed nonsense, it turns out that Dakota is the twin of Aubrey, whom the family bought from a crack addict when their own baby died in the hospital.

This revelation leads Dakota, via psychic twin telepathy, to the house of a serial-killing, fake-leg-enthusiast piano teacher who has been hacking up victims with his lovely blue-glass torture instruments for ages, because they didn't want him to teach them piano any longer. Are you with me so far? This girl really *is* Dakota Moss, twin sister to Aubrey Fleming, and has such a strong bond with this sister, whom she didn't even know existed until a day or two ago, that her appendages just started to fall off in the shower in sympathy with her. All caught up and befuddled? Good.

Dakota manages to kill the piano teacher, after chopping of his hand so that he can no longer play the piano (irony!), then uses her psychic visions to lead her to her twin, who is buried alive in a glass coffin, the whereabouts of which is confirmed by a very judgemental owl. When she finally releases her twin, you'd expect some kind of emotional reunion, an explanation, some questions. How do they feel about each other? What happens next? Will Dakota tell Aubrey that she totally touched her boyfriend on the toilet parts with her massive fake bionic man hand? Where will they live? Questions we all would like to have answers to, at the end of a film that has made no sense and thrown out more threads than a rave-dancing spider on crack. But if you're after closure, you're not going to find any here. Dakota finally smashes open the coffin, and the two girls simply lie on the ground and look up at the stars. It doesn't matter that Aubrey has been buried alive for at least a weekend and probably needs some kind of medical attention, or at the very least a drink of water. No questions are answered, no threads are tidied up. They just stopped filming. 'Make up your own bloody ending; we've run out of patience and the ability to care.'

Dealing with death is surprisingly easy

For many people, grieving is a process, and most know about the well-documented five stages: denial, anger, bargaining, depression and then acceptance. It is generally agreed that each person who experiences the death of a close friend or loved one will go through these stages as a coping mechanism to help them get over their loss. Unless, of course, that person is a character in a bad movie, when the stages of grieving are: shock, I'm fine, I'm more than fine, I'm horny, who wants pancakes?

Let us not forget that Ellen 'everybody I've ever met has been attacked by a shark' Brody in *Jaws The Revenge* moved to the Bahamas to get away from Amity because her son was eaten alive by a giant shark. Apart from having a bit of a wobble on a boat, she spends the rest of the movie acting as if she's not really that bothered by her loss. Although maybe the oddly incestuous relationship between her and her other son, Michael, is softening the blow. Maybe she isn't bothered about her shark-bait son Sean popping his clogs, because now she's got Michael all to herself. As well as her son Michael, she's also after Hoagie for a little having-fun-in-the-sun action. They go out dancing, drinking and giggling, and not a whiff of grieving shows on her face. (Yeah, you're right, that might be more to do with the actress's abilities than a character choice.) It seems all you need to get over your child dying horribly is a cocktail and the beach.

Films such as *Frankenfish* (2004), *House of the Dead* (2003) and *Bait* (2012) all feature characters who are picked off one by one by a killer, object or creature. It doesn't matter if it murders friends, family, enemies or strangers, in the same room, the same state or right next to them, the *laissez faire* attitude of a bad-movie characters to this carnage is to instantly forget they ever existed. The loss of a fellow protagonist is treated with the same level of distress as losing the car keys or a phone (or not even that; I think most of them would be more emotionally wrecked if their phone was to go missing). Never underestimate how quickly characters can bounce back in a bad movie, when there is a chance of a snog or a bit of sex-having, regardless of the zombie apocalypse happening outside their bedroom window. In Rob Cohen's *Daylight* (1996), Sylvester Stallone's character Kit watches multiple instances of carnage around him as a New York tunnel explodes and collapses. During the movie, he sees characters being picked off one by one, leaves a man to die alone, and barely survives the explosion that rockets him and fellow disaster movie fodder Madelyne (Amy Brenneman) through the water to the surface, where he bobs about unconsciously. After all of this, as he is being stretchered to the ambulance with Maddy, the two find the time to kid around, indulge in a bit of sexual tension and then joke that, on their first date, they should, 'take the bridge'. *Hahaha.* Hundreds of people died, now touch me where I pee. Sometimes I wish it were possible to talk to characters during moments like this. I could knock on the screen and ask them if they have any perspective. Sure, the lust for sex-having can be a strong one, but they could at least give it a few weeks after the death of a best friend/mother/brother before they get back on the sex-having bandwagon.

I've learned all these things and more from watching bad movies over the years. Of course, there have been other things: how to practise the art of slow-motion kung fu; how to use weaponry with pinpoint accuracy while having no formal training; how to fall in love and get married within the space of a week; how to say a glib line after killing a man; that story, music and dialogue don't necessarily need to match; that jumpers can be louder than talking; and that the entire internet uses only one password. I've also picked up a few interesting sex-having tips, but those are for a later chapter.

6
The Serious Business Of The Bad Comedy

Bad movies that start their lives as comedies rarely get included on *good* bad movie lists – and for sound reason. The theory here is that audiences enjoy a *good* bad movie because of their ability to see the intentionally unfunny morph into the unintentionally funny. For example, if a 'blow everything up and shoot all the bad guys' action movie such as *Commando* (1985) or a thrilling 'who is going to die next?' adventure/disaster movie like *Daylight* (1996) fails to hit the mark, it becomes laughable. We at least get some pleasure from it: the polar opposite response has been engaged in our brains, and now every over-the-top explosion, every character who pleads 'Just leave me behind' and every brave hero who is somehow able to run perfectly fine even though they've got multiple bone fractures and gunshot wounds, is entertaining. Discovering something that is unintentionally funny is like finding a rare gem, like a YouTube video of an evangelist Christian explaining that slavery is okay as long as it's handled in a respectful way, or of a kitten falling into a shoe. You enjoy the humour all the more because *you* found it; in some ways, you created it. But when a comedy isn't funny, and all the jokes are falling flat, it means the paper-thin plot becomes exposed to the audience and the awkwardness of bad humour creates an unwelcoming and unkind atmosphere. In short, it sucks ass.

When the intentionally funny morphs into being unintentionally unfunny, the film becomes inherently depressing. There aren't many things guaranteed to turn an atmosphere from fun to the kind of emotional state that makes you want to disappear into a large hole than a joke not landing or one that falls flat. It's that terrible moment at a dinner party where everybody is chatting and drinking and enjoying each other's company, and then a tipsy guest draws attention to himself and makes an ill-timed, slightly racist joke. In an instant, the room becomes silent, and people start fiddling with their cutlery and looking at their watches. Abruptly everybody remembers that they told their babysitter they wouldn't be late, and the room clears. But imagine if there were 200 people at that dinner party, and then imagine if that lame and stupid joke lasted an hour and a half and you couldn't leave the room. What started out as awkward silence would turn, quickly, to anger and then violence as the urge to throw a chair at something increased. There is little to no joy to be found within the scenes of a badly-made comedy, only pain.

In my experience, people are more unforgiving of bad comedy than of almost anything else. You only have to look at live stand-up comedy to see that. Even when presented with one of the worst plays, an audience will simply wait for an opportune moment and then leave the theatre; it takes a comedy club audience only a few seconds to decide that a comedian is unfunny before they start shouting or throwing ashtrays. I've seen it happen to a compere at a 'pop-up' comedy club in North London; first came the shouting, then came the ice cubes and last came three ashtrays. People are more likely to forgive a bad action or bad horror movie than they are a bad comedy. Is your superhero movie not quite super or heroic enough for you? Is *Green Lantern* (2011) not hitting the spot? Then why not give *The Green Hornet* (2011) a go, or just wait a few weeks; I'm sure Hollywood has yet another comic-book movie coming out. Comedy is a completely different ball game. There was a time when Eddie Murphy was at the top of his game, bringing out buddy comedy film after buddy comedy film. He started strong with *48 Hours* (1982), then kept the momentum going with *Beverly Hills Cop* (1987) and *Coming to America* (1988), before he went and hit a bit of wobble with *Holy Man* (1998). A few wrong turns here and there meant that by the time *Norbit* (2007) came around, nobody wanted to go anywhere near his movies, and the phrase 'Eddie Murphy comedy' became something of an oxymoron. It's a similar story with Steve Martin. The star of *The Jerk* (1979) used to be synonymous with innovative comedy, but now the mention of his name just reminds us all that he made *The Pink Panther 2* (2009), becoming a shadow of his former comedy box office winning self.

One of the reasons why comedy films are so hard to get right could be that comedy is constantly evolving, whereas other genres stay pretty much the same. A science fiction film from the 1950s is, narratively speaking, no different from a science fiction movie of today. The main difference is that the special effects look bit more homemade in the earlier movies. Society's taste for comedy, however, moves around. First it's slapstick, then it's satire, then it's farce, then it's dark comedy, then it's back to slapstick. Its constant motion means that when filmmakers manage to hit the target and produce a successful comedy it is, for the most part, down more to luck than to judgement.

It doesn't help that comedy is also subjective. I sometimes hear men bemoaning the fact that, while their friends find them hilarious, women just aren't interested. They conclude that when women claim they are looking for a guy with a sense of humour, this is just something they say but don't mean. On the contrary, I love men with a sense of humour, but it has to be a sense of humour that matches mine. If you're going to take me out and tell me knock-knock jokes all night, I'm going to find you incredibly annoying and change my mobile number the minute I get home. If you are in any doubt that comedy is subjective and hangs on personal taste, take the career of Adam Sandler. For many years, Sandler's films have been lamented by critics and comedy fans; many people who saw *Jack and Jill* (2011), on purpose, and had to sit there watching Sandler parade around the screen in drag, will tell you that it was one of the worst films of the year. It may also have been the first movie in history to sweep every single category at the Razzie Awards in 2012. But, to date, it has made over $150 million worldwide, so regardless of the reviews and Adam Sandler's past comedy turkeys, people watched it and enjoyed it and will continue to watch his movies. There will always be somebody somewhere who thinks his movies are funny; a close friend of mine thought *Spanglish* (2004) was a laugh riot; but we don't speak to each other as much as we used to ... because that guy is clearly an idiot.

I should make clear that as I go on to talk about specific bad comedy movies, I am not just focusing on the comedies that fall flat for me personally. It is possible to study comedy objectively and understand that, while I don't find a particular movie funny, it doesn't mean others will share the same opinion. As the saying goes, one man's *The Nutty Professor II: The Klumps* (2000) is another man's *Annie Hall* (1977). What I am looking at are the kind of movies where the inclusion of the word 'comedy' in the genre description provokes loud exclamations of surprise and possibly an e-mail to the Trading Standards Agency.

Let's take the movie *Crocodile Dundee Lost in Los Angeles* (2001) as an example of a movie that was billed as a comedy but managed to get through an entire 92 minutes without managing to raise a smile. What it did, however, was call into question the comedy validity of the rest of the *Crocodile Dundee* franchise. We once showed *Lost in Los Angeles* in Glasgow as part of the film/comedy festival, and our event had to be delayed because the 35mm print had been vandalised by whoever had shown it before us. No doubt some projectionist had been made to watch the whole thing multiple times when it was first in cinemas. Not only had they drawn a line through the first twenty minutes with a chinagraph pencil, which had to be delicately cleaned off by our projectionist, they had also written 'Crocodile Dundee is a twat' at the start, and busied themselves along a metre of the film stock drawing and colouring in Australian objects like a hat with corks on, a kangaroo and a can of beer, and then writing, 'This can fuck Mick Dundee up the ass' next to them. When a projectionist cries out for help in this way, you know that you're dealing with a very bad film. And it is. We should have heeded the warning and thrown it into the river Clyde.

The movie starts with our eponymous hero Crocodile Dundee

(Paul Hogan) and fellow crocodile hunter Jacko (Alec Wilson) forced up a tree by a giant crocodile that has eaten both of their boats. We should know from aeons of shark movies how much water-dwelling creatures love to eat boats. This is the opening joke. They are two crocodile hunters forced up a tree by a big crocodile. It was also the first joke to fall flat in Glasgow and cause the room to feel a little colder. Lamenting the fact that the crocodile hunter is now being reduced to nothing more than a dwindling tourist attraction, the two protagonists head off home to their respective plot devices, but not before Dundee has picked his son up from school and hypnotised a wild boar. Of course, there was no reason for the filmmakers to remind us that he does that hypnotising animals trick – unless, of course, it is necessary for the plot later in the movie ...

After this recap of his outback powers and a conversation that lets us know he's spawned a child, Dundee finally makes it home. There, his wife gets a phone call from her dad about some mystery to do with one of his newspaper groups, and now she has to go to Los Angeles and do some work for him. There's no reason to stay in Australia, where Mick is comfortable and understands the culture, so off they all go to the bright lights of LA – you know, just like in the last film, except you can't really say it's the same, because this time it's the other side of America. As soon as the jet takes off, you can hear audiences excitedly hoping that Mick Dundee will get embroiled in as many misadventures as possible where he confuses things for other things because he doesn't fully understand that things look slightly different in different countries. Comedy gold.

To cut a laboriously unfunny story short, he goes to LA, and it's very much the LA that we all know and love; his limo driver is an aspiring writer/director, everybody wants to be in the film industry and the women are either hotter than home or a car crash on legs. Dundee gets a job working on an action film, where he gets easily confused by things, and then he unwittingly uncovers a plot to use the studio to smuggle stolen paintings into the country and probably drugs as well. We learn that Aussies are tough men, American media types are wet and probably gay, and American women are chatty but they do have nice arses.

If you want to make the film a bit more bearable, there is a drinking game you can play; all you have to do is take a shot or a big gulp of drink whenever Dundee's annoying son says 'cool'. The booze will help to numb the pain; but, even better, the kid says it so many times that by the forty-fifth minute you will have passed out. Bliss.

The comedy is straining to emerge from the fish-out-of-water scenarios that have gone before; and that's the problem, we've seen them all before. There's only one thing worse than a joke that isn't that funny, it's a joke that is less funny now because it wasn't that funny the first time you heard it. For example, Mick and Jacko stop for a burger at Wendy's. When the server asks for his order, Mick calls her Wendy. You see, he's not from America, he's from a small town in Australia, so he thinks the server at Wendy's is Wendy. That is priceless. How about this one? In another scene, Mick stares at a Picasso painting the same way a dog swivels its head when its owner asks if it wants a sausage. After staring for a little while, he gives up and says that he's been drunk before, but he's never been that wasted. Do you see? He's from the outback, so the concept of cubist art is lost on him, and he thinks that Picasso painted a rubbish picture because he was drunk. It's the same joke! And it keeps on going. Later in the film, he causes a massive pile-up on an LA freeway as he stops to help a skunk in distress. Obviously the scene could be misconstrued as heart-warming, so to add more comedy, the filmmakers throw in the idea of people mistakenly believing that Mick is wandering the freeway holding a bomb. The miscommunication causes a dozen police cars, helicopters and cops with their guns drawn to face off with him. But that's not it, it gets funnier: the news reporters also thinks that he is holding his son hostage. He's not; it's just a misunderstanding, it's just him and his son having a walk along one of the busiest roads in California because they don't understand how traffic works, even though Mick has lived in New York, home of traffic. The police put down their weapons when they realise their mistake, and one old cop yells to his colleagues that everything is fine; Mick is not holding a bomb, he's holding a cat. But when they spot it's not a cat, it's a skunk, they panic and point their guns at it again. Forget terrorists; skunks are the real threat here.

The whole thing is just depressing, not just because the comedy is forced and hackneyed, but because the film doesn't really know what it wants to be. They've called it a comedy but, just like the rest of us, they've had no faith in it as a comedy vehicle, and so have rammed in a pointless action plot. The result is a movie that is less than the sum of its parts.

The comedy may be altogether depressing, but nothing could prepare you for the abject woefulness of the ending, which sees Dundee and Jacko stuck on a film set being chased by the bad guys. They all find their way onto a jungle set, where Mick is standing next to an empty cage doing something odd with his hands. The lion has escaped, and it's only Mick's famous 'point your finger at an animal and they won't attack you move' (ahhh, there's the reason for that scene at the start) that is keeping it still. The bad guys can't shoot Dundee, as then he wouldn't be able to do his hypnotising animals trick, and one of the jungle's most ferocious creatures would be released into the room. Except that this lion isn't ferocious, it's barely able to move, and when the pitiful thing's filmed from behind, all you can see are its bones sticking out of its fur. This king of the jungle is, at best, the 'grandfather' of the jungle, and at worst the 'six weeks to live' of the jungle. You have to see it to believe it, but they managed to find the rattiest, skinniest and most depressed-looking lion to wheel out as a threat, and it's not surprising that Dundee's Dr Doolittle hypnotic trick is working on it. I could probably keep its attention by waving a cushion. It would have to be a bright cushion, though, because it looks as though the lion has glaucoma; and I would have to wave it gently, as it appears the creature might shit itself if startled. The loud and powerful roar that comes out of it looks suspiciously like a yawn that's been overdubbed, and the red mark on its side where the filmmakers obviously shot the tranquilliser dart doesn't do much to negate my theory that this lion is stoned off its old and saggy tits.

The predictability of the movie's narrative and humour can

weigh heavy on an audience, as it wrings out all the joy of being surprised. They already know the jokes, they already know the plot, and they've already figured out after the opening titles that Mick Dundee is going to save the day, probably using his super mystical outback bullshit. There are questions that go through your mind as you watch it. Why did they bother making it? Why does it feel as though the movie is psychologically dragging me through rough terrain full of meaningless cul-de-sacs and broken glass? Where can I buy a chinagraph pencil?

Crocodile Dundee Lost in Los Angeles is a perfect example of why bad comedies struggle to be *good* bad movies. It's predictable, annoying and annoyingly predictable. But there are actually bad movies that reach a level below the unfunny comedy, and it's a well-worn level, littered with the most base humour and the most one-star reviews. The badly-made comedy parody movie genre. These movies live in a cold and unforgiving terrain, especially when what it is being parodied is a movie that was of dubious quality in the first place; this genre is pretty much the bottom of the comedy ladder

Nobody seeks out a modern spoof movie with an expectation of seeing BAFTA-winning performances and an interesting plot, but surely there has to be some semblance of effort and execution put into its creation, right? I wouldn't be so sure. The parody or spoof has most certainly become one of the laziest of all the cinematic genres. These movies don't need any imaginative scriptwriting, they just sit on top of an already-existing cultural product and suck it dry, like some parasitic bug gorging on hackneyed plots and one-dimensional characters. As long as they keep trotting out more pop culture references than you can shake a stick at, and enough fart jokes to keep a *Family Guy* audience satisfied, they'll make their intended audience of, predominantly, teenage boys very happy. If, according to the binary opposite theory, a bad movie is made good by virtue of it becoming an accidental parody, then watching a bad movie that is *already* a parody but supposedly a comedy should create enough bad movie science to make a black hole. But unlike the kind of black hole you might be familiar with, this one just sucks out any and all life from the film, steals your hopes and aspirations and strips you of your humanity.

What makes modern-day parody comedy movies particularly hard to watch is the fact that history has shown us that it is actually possible to do a parody that is clever, quick-witted and funny. Look at *Airplane!* (1980), *Spaceballs* (1987) and *The Naked Gun: From the Files of Police Squad* (1988). I'd even throw *Hot Shots* (1991) into the mix. These movies were cleverly-crafted comedies made to satirise specific film genres, and not hastily-thrown-together cash-ins. More importantly, they stayed within the remit of the films they were satirising. The modern-day parody, on the other hand, flip-flops from film to film, genre to genre, and adds television, music and internet memes until no subject is untouched and no real target is sighted. Some of these travesties put this right into their title, like the terrible Craig Moss movie *The 41-Year-Old Virgin Who Knocked Up Sarah Marshall and Felt Superbad About It* (2010). Which is all title and no film. (There is actually a film, but the negative worth of the film means that it, technically, doesn't exist.)

The most damning example of how modern-day parody movies can't even be bothered to parody the movies they put in their title is the Jason Friedberg and Aaron Seltzer film *Disaster Movie* (2008). In fact Friedberg and Seltzer are responsible for creating a number of these slapdash spoofs. Starting off as writers of the *Scream* parody *Scary Movie* (2000), they went on to write and direct *Date Movie* (2006), *Epic Movie* (2007), *Meet the Spartans* (2008), *Vampire Movie* (2010) and *The Starving Games* (2013); and at the time of writing they are in production on *Who the F#@k Took My Daughter*. That's almost a movie every year; if that doesn't scream 'quality', I don't know what does.

If *Disaster Movie* had been made to the same standard as the classic parody movies of the past, then it could have been a clever spoof, lambasting any one of the big-budget, high-profile disaster films of the last fifty or so years. At the very least it could have combined the clichéd aspects of each of them to create a mockery of the genre as a whole. But the filmmakers couldn't even be bothered to do that. The movie starts off in 10,001 BC (probably when most of its jokes were first written), with a caveman running away from a predator. After his face is trodden into a massive pile of poop – big poop; that makes it extra funny – he is hit by a pugil stick wielded by a character representing, I presume, somebody from the *American Gladiators* television show. Now our caveman is fighting a round of *American Gladiators*, for which I can find no good reason other than it was an easy pop reference for the audience to get. But we don't have to wait very long for another pop reference to stop by, as along comes a drunk Amy Winehouse (Nicole Parker), complete with large fangs and bad teeth, because she is British and the British have bad teeth. If your gnashers aren't white enough to outshine the sun, you are one of life's losers. Out from her hair comes an Apple laptop, on which she can check her Facebook – I'm sorry, 'Facenook' – and it is here she reveals to our caveman that apparently the world is going to end in 2008. Then she does a big long burp, which makes our caveman's dreadlocks flutter in the wind. Burping is funny, especially big burps, because it's wind coming out of us from inside of us and sometimes it smells like what we've just eaten. Why aren't you laughing? Are you dead inside or something?

I'm not the sort of person who demands historical accuracy – I don't mind a 20th Century hem on a 17th Century dress when watching a period drama – but what the hell does any the first six minutes of the film have to do with disaster movies? The only justification I can think of for this pointless opening is that it gives the filmmakers an opportunity to cram in as many 'youth references' as possible, to keep those under the age of 18 from being distracted by their iPhones. The idea seems to be that youngsters are more likely to lose interest in the movie if something on the screen isn't pandering to their inability to recognise cultural events that happened more than six months ago. As if to emphasise further the pointlessness of the opening six minutes, it turns out it was all a dream – which is the lamest of all movie expositions. When we do actually get to the point, it turns out that the film is about a meteor shower that is set to destroy the Earth but can be avoided with the help of a Crystal

Skull. What then follows is a relentless and random targeting of television shows and films such as *My Super Sweet 16 Party*, *Sex and the City*, *Juno*, *Enchanted*, *Hellboy*, *Alvin and the Chipmunks*, *Night at the Museum*, *Kung Fu Panda* and *Indiana Jones*, along with superheroes and even Sarah Silverman's song 'I'm Fucking Matt Damon'.

One of the few references to actual disaster movies is a nod to *The Day After Tomorrow* (2004) when the city starts to freeze, but that's about it. The movie might as well have been called *Random Popular Culture References Loosely Based Around a Weak Story ... Oh, and People Have Wind*. The comedy doesn't come from anything original and would have the same laugh quota if a person stood in front of the camera, held up a picture of somebody famous and pointed to it saying, 'Hey, remember when they did that thing? Funny, wasn't it?' For two hours. Not many things are as depressing as a dull and badly-made movie, very few things are as depressing as a dull and badly-made comedy movie, and *nothing* is as depressing as a dull and badly-made cash-in comedy parody movie.

Sometimes, worse than a movie claiming to be a comedy and disappointing an audience to epic proportions, is when filmmakers incorporate inept comedy into another genre of movie. A typical example is the inclusion of a leading character with a supposedly amusing trait, such as an annoyingly confident protagonist who offers nothing but glib lines following the death of every bad guy, or a stereotypical dizzy blonde woman who is always confusing the simplest things by virtue of the Crocodile Dundee trait of not knowing that some things are different from other things. Worse still is the ultimate in pulling focus and annoying an audience, the completely pointless comedy character. How I hate these. I always hope they will be quickly killed off, and yet they never are. It can be stressful enough watching a bad movie without some smartarse gurning his or her way through the entire film, cracking jokes and trying to 'make light' of any and every situation. Get a grip, Roy, or whatever your name is; the entire boatload of tourists has capsized in shark-infested waters, nobody wants to hear your funny line about Noah's Shark. Each stupid remark made by the pointless comedy character cuts through me like a knife, or like Hulk Hogan's acting in … well, in every single movie Hulk Hogan has ever been in.

The best, or worst, example of the needless inclusion of a comedy sidekick is the character Jimmy Sands, played by Leon (yup, just the one name), in the Louis Morneau-directed Lou Diamond Phillips vehicle *Bats* (1999). I am assuming that you all can tell from the title what kind of film *Bats* is, even if you have never seen it. It's treading familiar creature-feature territory, with mutated killer bats causing havoc in a small town and threatening to obliterate the population. The bats attack, just like many other lower-budget creatures do, by looking like a rubber toy, flying in as if thrown by a runner and having their victims hold them to their own neck, head, leg etc until they are dead (the people, that is, not the bats). But more annoying than people being out-acted by fake killer bats is Jimmy Sands – who sounds like he should be a beach resort for couples only – and his constant jive-talking rhetoric, which actually makes me yearn to hear the other characters talk about the plot. I'd rather listen to Lou Diamond Phillips' hero talk about how a makeshift electric fence is going to save them all than to Sands and his distracting retorts to every single bloody thing he is told to do. For example, he's working with a bat expert, yet every time he is asked to do something bat-related, it comes as a complete surprise to him, and he complains about it, because doing bat stuff is yucky, he ain't got time for that shit. You are working with a bat expert; what did you expect to be doing? He even utters the painfully clichéd 'Houston, we have a problem' when things go tits up. And it isn't as if fear and a need to break the tension slowly develop him into an annoying character; he's off-the-charts annoying from the very first scene.

That first scene opens with Dr Shelia Casper (Dina Meyer) squeezing through some tight hidey holes in search of bat roosts. It's dark and it's craggy and it probably has a very strong smell of ammonia, and Jimmy offers words of comfort through the intercom with phrases like 'Rather you than me' and 'If it's too tight, turn around and come out, because you do not want to rely on me to get your ass back up here.' Why not? Isn't that the entire point of you being there, Jimmy? What other jobs did you get fired from before you had this one? 'Hey, I hope you're a really good swimmer. Don't let the lifeguard uniform fool you, I can't even swim, so don't rely on me to save your drowning ass from a shark attack.' And it continues like that for the entire opening scene. When squashing through a tight space, Casper quips that she should lay off the cheesecake, to which Jimmy replies, 'You talking to a brother. You know I don't mind a little extra weight, especially if it's in the right place.' At one point, she asks him a valid question (the same one I asked): if he hates bats and caves so much, why is he in the middle of the desert on a mountain with her, studying them? His response is that he is there because she is 'kinda cute'. That's how I keep all of my jobs; I tell my boss that I hate what I do, and that I'm only there because I want to stare at their sweet ass all day. It's a shame that Jimmy is not a fan of bats up close. If he were, then he could be lured to a cave, and with a few sticks of dynamite we could solve the bat problem and the Jimmy Sands problem at the same time.

His chattering stupidity carries on way after the opening scene; in fact, right the way through the movie. When an investigator introduces himself as a representative from the CDC – Centre for Disease Control – his reply is, 'Hey, I never touched that girl.' *What?* I'm not sure I know what the joke even means. Does he think he's responsible for chlamydia on a global scale? During the autopsy on the first bat victim, his reaction is to tell everybody, 'Keep doing what you're doing,' before running out of the room to throw up. He has a weak stomach, probably because he's just read the rest of the script. On discovering another dead bat victim: 'This definitely isn't going to look good in the morning paper.' After being attacked by a swarm of bloodthirsty bats: 'I'm thinking about heading to Antarctica right about now. I checked into this; there ain't one bat up there, cos they hate the cold.'

During the post-bat carnage clean-up of the entire town, Jimmy and the rest of the Scooby gang remain after the place has been evacuated. When they break the news to Jimmy that they are all staying, his reply is, 'You got to be pulling my leg, because this shit is not funny'. No, Jimmy, it's not funny, it's bloody exasperating. And it goes on and on, over and over again: set-up, weak punchline, set-up, weak punchline, set-up, attitude and then weak punchline. I am sure that the intention was for his lines to provide some kind of comic relief. But it's not relief; it just adds further to the frustration of the already questionable plot and even more questionable puppet bats. If I start to watch a film and one character stands out as a quick-talking quip-maker, my heart sinks, because I know the film is going to drag. Bad movie + bad character + bad jokes = boredom ∞.

Like I said earlier, comedy is subjective, and there are going to be people who like their comedies a bit stupid or a bit slapstick or a bit childish, and those films will always find their audience. However, a bad comedy, one that fails to deliver on any level – and I'm talking *Sex Lives of the Potato Men* (2004) bad – will always break whatever delicate magic spell that enables a terrible movie to cross over to the other side. There is no afterlife for a bad comedy movie, just death. And if filmmakers think they are going to breathe life into a film by bringing comedy elements into it, with the intention of covering two genre bases at once, they are mistaken. What they are actually doing is unleashing a virus into their movie, a virus that will slowly and painfully kill it. It would certainly seem that as far as *good* bad movies go, comedy is the equivalent of joy Kryptonite.

7
The Guide to Bad Sex-Havers

I'm sure that most people who have seen up to ten films in their lives can agree that sex-havers are a dangerous breed of people. If you're a main character in a film, you want to stay clear of sex-havers and of indulging in sex-having yourself. If you're a secondary character and you find yourself sex-having, you had better prepare yourself for a rough ride; and, in truth, you probably aren't going to make it to the end of the movie. It doesn't matter if the scene is a bedroom where quiet jazz music plays and curtains billow in a soft night breeze as the female character wiggles and writhes about on the bellybutton of her male partner. It doesn't matter if they're sex-having in the back of a truck, where the female character wiggles and writhes about naked on the bellybutton of her fully-clothed male partner. And it doesn't matter if they're sex-having in a lake, where the female character wraps her legs around the male partner's bellybutton as a camera operator films shakily under the water. (Bellybutton sex seems to be a very popular sex position in movies; I can only imagine that every Hollywood actor has a very large 'outie'.) Whatever the setting, sex-havers attract bears, they attract sharks, they attract earthquakes, they attract giant snakes, and if the end of the world is nigh, no two ways about it, sex-havers are the cause.

When thinking, for this chapter, about the various sex-having scenes that have been, excuse the term, inserted into thousands of bad movies, and mainstream movies, I started to question why filmmakers have sex scenes at all. Why do we need them? What do they actually add to the narrative? I could live my life happily without seeing strangers, actors or otherwise, having sex on a screen in front of me. We know people have sex, and we know this because the Earth keeps getting populated, so why do we need to see it happen during a film about sharks or zombies or shark zombies? If it's not going to help save the city from the massive meteor heading toward it, I don't care about it. I brought this topic up in conversation with a few film-centric friends, and some of them took the predictable Hollywood stance that sex scenes are put in films to add some sizzle, to keep people's attention. But are they really that sexy? Has anybody reading this ever felt the urge to stop the action during the sex-having scene in *Jason Goes to Hell: The Final Friday* (1993) to go off and have a wank?

Another friend suggested that the sight of sex-havers might titillate a few, predominantly male, members of the audience. It has been said before that sex scenes are placed in movies to keep men interested in the bits of a film that don't involve car chases and to perk them up by seeing boobs in those that do. But if your story is so bad that you need a pair of bouncy tits to keep people watching, maybe the porn industry would be a better fit. I didn't come out of the cinema after seeing *12 Angry Men* (1957) and think, 'That film was okay, but I would have been much more invested if the jurors had gotten naked and daisy-chained around the table.'

Boobs have always been synonymous with bad movies, B-movies and cult movies in general. Perhaps in the earlier days of the industry, just as the American New Wave was happening, filmmakers were overly excited by the newfound freedom to include shocking elements like blood, gore, blasphemy and boobies into their films. (*Blood, Gore, Blasphemy and Boobies* is definitely going to be the name of my first album when I form a band.) You can't get more anti-Doris Day than a few Russ Meyer films bouncing their bounty up and down the screen to that new-fangled rock guitar music. But surely now we have the internet, we can keep tits out of the movies?

The worst sex-having scenes are the ones where the sex-having appears out of nowhere; and it is especially awkward when it's in a film that I am watching with my parents. I know it's a well-worn topic – the embarrassment felt by a son or daughter, of any age, when placed a situation where sex-havers frolic naked on the screen, oblivious to the suffering they are causing. This is when you generally find yourself fiddling with an invisible piece of cotton on your trousers or getting up to make everybody a cup of tea. I've seen some movies with my folks that have warranted at least eight tea breaks, and at my age, my bladder can't handle it. In my house, however, it was never the embarrassment of naked people that made me dread sex-having scenes, it was the response of one particular family member. This was my grandmother. She was a big fan of the VHS serialised drama box-set when I was a kid, and one particular Sunday, as I recall, we were sitting down to watch another gritty working-class period drama about coal pits or factories or pie-making when two of the characters ran into a shed and started sex-having on a pile of Hessian sacks. The first thing my grandmother did was the classic old-woman shriek – you can hear it emanating from any bingo hall or Saga holiday around the world. Then she laughed a big, meaty Sid James laugh and said to me, 'I remember me and your grandpa did that in the coal shed once. My ass went as black as the night.' I was 11 at the time. My nightmare continued as the male sex-haver lifted the female sex-haver up against the wall, tits and corset all over the place. My grandmother then said, 'We couldn't do that because grandpa had a big one, so it would only go in so far.' I may have passed out. The hurt caused by that badly-made Northern drama eventually healed, but the emotional scars inflicted by my grandmother sharing intimate details about the girth of my grandfather's chappie will last forever.

Social and family embarrassment aside, I can't think of a sex-having scene in a movie that wasn't ridiculous and badly-put-together. I've never watched a couple of sex-havers on the big screen and thought, 'Oh, that looks like a natural and normal way to have sex, and not at all uncomfortable or awkward. I may just try that when I get home.' Sometimes they are too slick, too contrived, and there's always too much boob rubbing.

Seriously, people, can we stop with all the boob rubbing? The odd caress, sure, but don't rub up and down between them like you're applying vapour rub to a chest infection. If men (and sometimes women) aren't rubbing between the boobs, they are squeezing them and biting them as if they're testing fruit in a supermarket. Cut it out.

Women's smooth moves aren't let off that lightly during preposterous sex scenes either. Why in movies do women always want to rub their faces all over their man's stomach like they are looking for new and interesting ways to wipe a runny nose? What's on there that's so appealing? Maybe I'm missing out and there are a group of men who enjoy having women smell their tummy before smashing their face repeatedly into it. Men, stop rubbing between women's boobs; women, stop chafing your face on men's bellies. Neither of you are being sexy, and you're just confusing future generations of actual sex-havers who are going to be childless with chafed boobs and stomachs.

I should make it clear that I'm not against movies including sex-having scenes that are integral to the plot. I can't even imagine what *Showgirls* (1995) would be like without the dolphin-like hair-whipping and body-splashing sex scene between Elizabeth Berkley and Kyle MacLachlan. Or the rhythmic bouncing in the strip club that makes him do some sex wee in his pants. The sex in that film belongs there, because that is what Berkley's character does; she's a stripper, an erotic dancer, a woman working in the sex industry, so of course she is going to be having sex. The same goes for *Fifty Shades of Grey* (2015) or *The Secretary* (2002). Both of those movies feature sex-having almost as much as the other scenes that are progressing the story, and it needs to be seen. It would be a pretty strange film if every other scene in *Fifty Shades* had the main protagonists coming out of a different location, doing up their clothes and saying, 'Wow, I very much enjoyed that kinky sex we just had in there, especially the bit where you tied me to the headboard and put those ping pong balls up into my bum hole. Let's do it again in 13 minutes' time.'

Diary of a Sex Addict (2001) is a great sex-based movie, and another classic from the Nu Image film camp – which proves that they have more to their canon than prehistoric sharks, giant spiders and migraine-inducing action movies. It is a badly-conceived kitchen-sink drama about a family man who is a raving nymphomaniac on the side, and it brings the sexploitation genre into a newer, classier, more noir environment – or at least it tries to. This movie even stars a real actress, Rosanna Arquette, from the Arquette family – you know the ones, they are a bit like the Baldwins, but odder and with bigger teeth. Supposedly this is a serious film about sex addiction. The sultry DVD cover art may lure you into thinking that it is full of classy sex scenes, all integral to the plot, shot in deep focus, with shadowy mood lighting, on crisp white sheets. The reality is that it is a long bus ride away from being classy. Watching a pensioner try to get egg out of their dentures with a bit of cardboard would be sexier than its sex-having scenes. That is not to say that pensioners can't be sexy; I'm sure they can be, to other pensioners. What I'm saying is that egg stuck between slack dentures is way more sexy than anything *Diary of a Sex Addict* can muster.

Amongst the clumsy, shaky, low-quality, iPhone-style footage, audiences will find an Aladdin's cave full of every type of sex-having you can shake a stick at – but no stick sex; sorry, stick enthusiasts, get your own niche. The sex-having is so unsexy, so ridiculous and upsetting that it might put you off sex-having for a while. As I was watching the film with my good buddy Joe, we both laughed and wept simultaneously at the preposterousness of what we were seeing, and for the fact that we had actually paid money to be shown it.

The movie sets the ludicrous tone from the get-go. About five minutes in, there is an unusual scene in a restaurant between a mysterious lady and Billy Idol's dad lookalike and sex addict Sammy Horn (Michael Des Barres). Yes, Horn, Sammy Horn. No, I didn't just make that up; that's the character's real name. I know it's a terrible name, and you know it's a terrible name, but clearly the people who made the film thought they were being frightfully clever. Little Miss Sultry Knickers (or No Knickers, as it later transpires) leads Mr Horn into the men's bathroom, offering him a surprise. I don't want to spoil it for anybody, but the surprise is that when she takes her coat off, she is naked underneath. I understand that people like to keep their sex-having spicy by adding different positions and new locations – people can sex-have wherever they want – but why choose a men's bathroom? I understand that cottaging in public toilets has been a popular activity since the invention of the purpose-built amenities, but a quick nosh through a glory hole is a bit different from utilising the entire space of the bathroom for full naked sex-having. Imagine stripping naked and perching your ass on any surface in a men's bathroom. Are you imagining it? Now do you feel like you want to take a shower? I don't want to venture into a men's public bathroom fully clothed, never mind with my most vulnerable openings exposed to the elements. Surely it has to take at least some of the sexy shine off an intimate moment when you're knee deep in urine-filled floor water or sitting on a bacteria-ridden sink trying to be alluring as the stench of man poop wafts around you like a scatological Bisto advert. But this mysterious woman loves it, and as the sex-having plays out, it is obvious that she loves it a little *too* much.

As soon as Mr Horn positions himself behind her, she starts to scream. She's not just moaning or being loudly appreciative, she is actually screaming. At this point, you'd hope that a sensible man would stop to check that his gentleman's sausage hadn't been magically replaced with a pointed steel spike during the night. But nope, he keeps on keepin' on. Unexpected screaming aside, what makes this scene particularly noteworthy is the fact that the filmmakers have chosen to intersperse the sex-having and the screams of, let's call it, passion with a series of oddly-chosen cutaways. These range in strangeness from the restaurant clientele fleeing the venue in fear of their lives, clearly believing that there is a killer at work in the bathroom, to our mysterious screaming sex-haver smashing mirrors with her fists and deploying the wall-mounted soap pump in the throes of ecstasy. She is even so careless that she pushes over a small plastic bin. The scene ends when the bar owner calls the police to inform them that somebody is being murdered in the men's room, and the two sex-havers are both arrested. If I had been making the movie, apart from ensuring it made more sense, I would have improved the comedy value of that scene by the inclusion of a small, bald, fat guy emerging from one of the cubicles looking slightly embarrassed as the police lead the sex-havers away.

Later on in the film, after many and varied, but all equally confusing and brain-numbing, sexual encounters, Mr Horn finds himself in bed with the same mystery lady, only this time she is wearing nothing but a stocking over her head. I don't know why; maybe she came to him immediately after holding up a post office. The only saving grace here is that they are sex-having on a bed, and that bed is in a bedroom and not in a furniture shop. She aggressively leaps about on top of him, screaming (of course she is, that's her thing); but instead of garbled noises, this time she is screaming that she is a bitch and a whore. I'm not sure about the validity of her self-deprecation, but she certainly shows no respect to the tensile strength of your average queen-size bed, as she bounces and gyrates about with free abandon.

After a few more moments of sporadic gesticulations, she yells 'I'm coming', and is immediately tossed aside, still screaming, by Mr Horn. You'd think he too would be indulging in the over-the-top sexual gymnastics and accompanying screeches of passion, but instead he looks rather relieved to get the fitting Tasmanian Devil off his penis – which, I assume, is now red-raw and probably a little bit broken. I asked Joe if this was the sort of thing that men wanted in bed, and he told me that there might be some men who enjoy having sex with a banshee bucking bronco, and then again there might be some who enjoy sticking their penis into an office fan or wanking with sandpaper, but that it wasn't particularly common. He then explained that the normal way to have sex was the British way; the man on top thinking of horrible images to delay satisfaction, and the lady on her back thinking about tips she read earlier in *Take a Break* magazine.

You'd suppose that having sex with the human carwash would be the oddest part of the aforementioned scene, but no, as soon as she's off him, he's daydreaming about teaching his son to shave. Mr Horn does, at least, show himself as having some morals. Later in the film, for example, he has difficulty getting into a blow job from a hooker, because he's being observed by the face of Jesus on a candle. When you think about it, he's almost a saint.

If you're interested, and lord knows why you would be, the whole movie ends on a disappointing but predictably ambiguous note. Mr Horn's wife catches him sex-having with a couple of birds, they go to a sex-havers therapy session together, and he tells her he won't do it again as he nestles his creepy head on her cleavage. There is no real ending; but, to be fair, there isn't much of a beginning or a middle either.

Bad sex-having in good movies is lamentable enough, and so is bad sex-having in bad sex-focused movies, but what is even worse is bad sex-having in bad movies that are *not* sex-focused. Good movies with terrible sex scenes at least have the rest of the film to distract the audience, but bad movies don't have that luxury. The audience are already confused as to why the army would want to genetically modify a penguin to make the ultimate killing machine, so your crazy sex scene in the otter enclosure is really only going to exacerbate that confusion.

Take *Zombie Lake* (1981), the full-of-family-fun Nazi zombie movie. It's got dubbed-Italian-voice-acting badness, camera-operators-who-seem-to-have-had-no-balance-or-tripod-ability badness, zombie-make-up-that-has-come-straight-out-of-a-Tesco's-budget-Halloween-pack badness, and a crew-along-with-their-cables-are-seen-on-camera-almost-as-much-as-the-cast badness. The audience are already processing all of that, as well as asking themselves why the green on the zombie faces seem to be coming off in the underwater shots, why the zombies are dribbling blood onto the necks of their victims, and whether or not it would it be possible to pitch a 'my dead Nazi zombie dad' sitcom based on the scene where a daughter and her zombie father enjoy a day in the park. (I would totally watch that sitcom.) The audience will probably have already worked out that the blond Nazi is the father of the creepy-eyed child-of-the-corn character; but just to hammer the point home, the filmmakers have kindly included an elongated sex scene in the farmyard barn.

I wish directors and writers would stop setting sex scenes on hay-bales in barns. For one thing, that's some animals' food; they don't need sex-havers' bodily excretions leaking all over it and flattening it out. How would you feel if you were served a steak covered in ass-prints and jizz? Secondly, and this may just be me being nit-picky, if you're going to do some sex-having, why on earth would you do it in a barn full of rusty, pointy, septicaemia-causing objects? Perhaps all of the sex-having in barns and hay is how mad cow disease spread. There are so many tools and rusted knickknacks adorning the sex barn in *Zombie Lake* that I feel I should have a tetanus shot each time I watch it. This is also another movie with a lot of neck kissing and boob rubbing. The sex scene adds nothing to the story, unless it serves as a moral for the audience – the moral being that if you have sex before marriage, you'll turn into a Nazi zombie or die in childbirth. Which could be a positive message of abstinence to some, and a catalyst for sex-having to others.

Zombie Lake features a lot of shirtless women running away from, or being attacked by, the Nazi zombies. This is only to be expected; there is a long B-movie tradition of scantily-clad women rushing about the place. Having pillow fights naked and running away from axe murderers naked are common inclusions. There is a great scene near the middle of *Zombie Lake* where a busload of lady volleyball players drive up to the lake for a bit of cooling off – at least, I think they are volleyball players, as they have some kind of a ball with them, although from the crude construction and decoration of the beaten-up van they arrive in, they could just as easily be a cargo of East European trafficking victims. The girls giggle and prance out of the van, as women in movies so often do, and off they pop for a naked swim in the lake. No inhibitions, no cursory glances, it's off with the clothes, out with the vaginas and into the water. I've lost count of the number of times I've been hanging out in a beat-up old van with my friends and thought, *Let's get our tits out and splash about for a bit.* This scene is more like a documentary to me than a work of fiction. And it doesn't have to be a lake, it could just as easily be a restaurant or a shopping centre or even a ride at Alton Towers. Whenever us girls get together in groups of four or more, we grapple our whaps out and fanny about for a bit.

I blame romantic comedies and sitcoms for creating a whole generation of men who think that girls get naked during sleepovers, eat ice cream, practise kissing and talk about guys, instead of what most of us really do, which is wear comfy trousers and shove as many doughnuts into our faces as we can. Although, having said that, something similar did once happen to me when I was in my early twenties. But if you think this is the part of the book that gets all sexy and Sapphic, you can think again; the whole experience still leaves me cold.

Work had organised a team-bonding trip to the swimming pool so that, as a reward for our hard work over the summer, we could take a refreshing dip after a long day stuck in a stuffy, hot office. We dived in, splashed about (with our tits placed firmly placed inside our swimming costumes at this point), and after an hour or so made our way back to the dressing cubicles. We all chatted our way to our respective gender changing rooms, and my boss stayed with me as I headed for my locker. I turned my key in the locker door, retrieved my bag and towel, and when I closed the locker door, there was my boss, stark naked in front of me with her bathing costume in her hand. Being confronted by unexpected pubic hair is one thing, but being confronted by unexpected pubic hair on a woman who had hired me and was responsible for my pay packet, not to mention the lottery syndicate, was unsettling; remarkably so.

It can be a sharp shock when one is faced with guerrilla nudity, but to have shown how traumatised I was by the incident would have been rude, so I had to try to contort my face into a kind of *Yeah, this is a totally normal thing to be experiencing on a Tuesday* expression so as not to offend her. I was willing my eyes to stay above nipple line, which was actually rather easy, as the woman was in her sixties, so her nipples, seemingly given up on life, were slowly committing suicide from her chest and were somewhere just north of her belly button. Despite my best efforts, my eyes betrayed me, just the once, and I took in her Full Monty as we turned the corner, walking toward where the empty changing cubicles were located. Obviously being an older lady, she spent her time maintaining her actual garden, not her lady garden, so her *personal enclosure* looked like a tufty tepee made out of wire wool and eiderdown.

However, at no point during our discussion was there any hint of a pillow fight or a playful push into the hand-dryer. We talked until we got to our destination, then we got changed, and I never asked her why the hell she thought it was okay to strip off just metres from the safety of a lockable changing room. Maybe it's the fault of those early nudist documentary films that showed carefree naked men and women laughing and playing tennis in the buff.

More often than not, if you're sex-having in a creature-feature or a horror movie then you're a sure-fire target for attack, and one or both of you are going to end up as food or fertiliser. Nothing says 'mutilated bodies found strewn around the living-room by a member of the family' more than a couple of sex-havers on film. That goes double for sex-havers who are sex-having *al fresco*. It's a red flag that signals a particular lack of morals (they probably aren't married either, or at least not to each other), which grants the audience permission to sit back and enjoy them dying. Vice and sex-having have always been targets on your back, and every generation has had its own punishable behaviour, be it cigarette-smoking, alcohol-drinking, drug-doing or exhibiting questionable moral character. People remember the shower scene from *Psycho* (1960), for example, but few remember the reason why Marion Crane (Janet Leigh) had to die in the first place: she was a thief, a common office rat who stole $40,000 from her company's client and then went on the run. Hitchcock couldn't let her live; what sort of a message would that send to kids? That it's okay to steal? Best they be told that if they did steal, they would be set upon in the shower by a transsexual with a bloody big knife.

While I'm writing about monsters, boobs and blood, it seems only proper to mention Roger Corman, 'King of the Bs' and the man responsible for some of the best/worst movies since the 1950s. A low-budget independent producer, director and actor who revels in the grotesque, he has brought to the screen some true classics of the cult movie circuit, including *Forbidden World* (1982), *Carnosaur* (1993) and the wonderful *Piranhaconda*(2012). The Carnosaur creature actually features in a bizarre sex scene in Corman's film *Raptor* (2001), which is partly made up of scenes taken from *Carnosaur* – something that can be disconcerting if you don't know this before you start watching it. The sex-havers in *Raptor* are minding their own business, sex-having in the back of a flat-bed truck (sex-having and outside, this is not a good sign), but it isn't the predictable 'naked woman bouncing on top of an almost fully-clothed man' for about eight minutes that makes this sex scene bad, it's that after the first few minutes, there seems develop a creeping feeling of *déjà vu*, and not just because most of the film has been lifted from another. Then it hits you: these sex-havers are on a loop. Shot after shot, you can almost direct the scene yourself: 'Action. Okay, you bounce up and down on his lap for a bit, show us your boobs, do a moan. Wide shot of the sex-havers. Bounce up and down on his lap for a bit, show us your boobs, do a moan. Wide shot of the sex-havers. Bounce up and down on his lap for a bit, show us your boobs, do a moan. Wide shot of the sex-havers. Cut.'

When films behave badly, I started to panic and put myself into odd philosophical situations. Here I posited that maybe time, and I, was stuck in a loop. Luckily for me, it turned out there was no time loop, just a lazy production decision to add some extra time and bouncing boobage to the movie. Needless to say, the couple's sex-having high is dampened by the arrival of a bloodthirsty dinosaur puppet, which chomps the guy and sprays him all over the outside of the truck. Not such a happy ending for him. It's just like the bit in *Anaconda* (1997) where Owen Wilson's character, Gary Dixon, takes a woman off into the jungle for a bit of sex-having but is interrupted by a wild boar and good old lumpy Jon Voight, who saves them from being gored to death. Unfortunately, no amount of sneering from Voight is going to absolve the sex-havers, and Dixon finds himself swallowed whole by a giant snake later on in the movie.

If you were to ask me what my favourite bad-movie sex scene of all time is, I would reply, 'That's a strangely forward question to ask a stranger,' but I'd answer you anyway. For the most emotionless, curious and pointless sex-having on screen, the award has to go to the Patrick Swayze classic *Road House* (1989). Thankfully, the rest of the film is sufficiently bad and over-the-top to be entertaining, so the audience don't have to dwell too long on the lack of on-screen chemistry between Swayze (Dalton) and co-star Kelly Lynch (Doc). A more perfunctory pairing of celluloid bromide has not been seen on the medium-size screen since the dalliances of Tom Cruise and Kelly McGillis in *Top Gun* (1986). We are made aware early on in the film of Dalton's ease in letting it all hang out, as witnessed during scenes where he's free-balling it out of bed and giving Carrie (Kathleen Wilhoite) a look at his buns of steel. Not to mention his penchant for topless tai-chi in the morning. It is damning indeed that he puts more passion into his slow-motion man-karate than his sex-having; but then again, he does live in a barn, where splinters are a real hazard, no matter how much he's renovated.

The pre-sex-having starts with Dalton searching the radio for some romantic music – you can't be sex-having in silence, that would be unacceptable. A few comically inappropriate tunes later, he comes across a perfect song that, luckily for us, has just started. It never ceases to amaze me how in movies the right song will always start at the beginning when you need to set a mood. Also, talk radio stations are conspicuous by their absence; nobody ever rolls over satin sheets and clicks on the radio to hear Dave from Telford moaning about how the council should do something about the potholes on the A548.

As sex-having is popular in real life as well as in the movies, I thought it might be helpful for me to give step-by-step instructions in the Dalton seduction technique, in case any men reading this wish to try it for themselves.

Step 1

Slowly back your prey, I mean lover, into a corner as you start to undress yourself. Make it subtle at first, like you are just following her over to the wall, chat a bit to her about her dead parents and lack of husband, but be sure to keep following her, wherever she walks. *Do not* take your eyes off her. She may start darting her eyes back and forth, probably looking for an escape route, but don't let this put you off. Just continue to guide her backwards like a sheepdog, until her only two options are to give in to your seduction technique while backed up against the rough wall, or dive out of the health and safety nightmare that is your giant open window.

Step 2

Look like you're about to kiss her, but don't; just stare at her face for a really long time. And I mean really long. You're going to want to make her feel uncomfortable and a little freaked out. But just go with it; the payoff will be both disappointing and upsetting.

Step 3

Hold her head. Women love it when men hold their heads in their giant meaty hands; it makes them feel safe. Having their head completely engulfed by a man's hands comes second only to a man taking hold of their chin. If you think about it, logically, what woman wouldn't want to be led around by the chin? It is what we all crave, as the chin is actually a woman's biggest erogenous zone. But, for this particular act of sex-having, we're going with the head-holding, so you're going to want to start at the back of the neck, bring your hands up and forward and then just wipe your hands all over her cheeks as if her skin were a hand towel. Remember, you're still just staring at your lover/date /girlfriend/inflatable, and you're still not talking. Uncomfortable is the new sexy.

Step 4

Grab some other part of your partner, any part will do, and start to sway her back and forth in time with the music; gently at first, but gradually more noticeably, before going in for the semi kill. This involves *almost* kissing, but still not actually kissing. You want to breathe all over her, put your mouth right by hers so that they are nearly touching, but don't actually touch them together. Instead, what you're going to do is just pant your hot, nasty breath on her as you stare, questioningly, into her eyes. Still no touching. Still no kissing. You want to keep this up for as long as you can in order to make it patently obvious to all who are watching that there is no real sexual chemistry between the two of you, and neither of you are good enough at acting to mask that fact.

Step 5

Undo your trousers and then scratch her legs; really scratch them, put some welly into that thigh-skin scraping. Once her legs are thoroughly scratched and your trousers are totally undone but somehow not falling down, you can finally kiss your partner. But just the one kiss; you want to see your partner straining to pull your head toward her as you try to avoid any intimate contact that isn't strictly necessary. Of course she wants more; it's all the awkward staring, it works like a charm every time.

Step 6

Luckily for you, your partner isn't wearing any pants, so grab her ass and hoist her onto you, so that she can wrap her legs around your waist. Now the real fun starts. Even though you don't want to be kissing her mouth, you do want to be attacking her neck like those disgusting tiny fish that eat the dead flesh of women's feet in shopping centres. You may need to get more purchase, so properly smoosh her up against the roughest stone wall you can find, and hold her there for a bit with the power of your groin.

Step 7

Be oblivious as to the nature of what you are doing. You may have started to have sex by the look of all the grinding up against that rough wall, but the acting is so bad that you could just be sanding her down to varnish later. Keep that air of mystery about you, and keep her guessing. Having your trousers on will add to the mystery. Is it in? Is it out? Who knows. During this time of possible sex-having, you may want to encourage your partner to make as many Kenneth Williams-in-a-*Carry On*-film-style faces as possible. Really, the more grotesque, the better. Duck face, pouty face, shock-at-waking-up-hungover-to-find-you've-signed-on-to-this-movie face, all of the classics. The only real way to stop her from all of the distracting face-pulling is to shove your fat tongue into her mouth. And don't be subtle about it, either; really ram it in there, like an anaconda forcing its blubbery head into a rabbit hole. That will wipe the daft look off her face. And replace it with a look of nausea.

Step 8

In the middle of thrusting about, during the ambiguity as to whether you are properly sex-having or, instead, indulging in good old-fashioned teenage dry humping, pick her up and carry her around the room. Sure, to the onlookers it would appear that you are showing her your newly-decorated apartment while she balances on your penis: 'Over here is where I keep the magazines, and over here are the sofa and chair I bought on eBay.' But you will know that it's all part of the sex-havers A-game, and after a few more stops around the barn, you can collapse onto the bed, safe in the knowledge that no further sex-having needs to be shown – which neatly avoids all the bumping and grinding and apologising you would so clearly have to do.

Step 9

Post coitus. Leave your lady wrapped up in a sheet; she'll be worn out from all the boob rubbing and obvious penis gymnastics you've been indulging in during the evening. Let her wake naturally and, as she has the decency to wrap herself up in a sheet, pay her the same consideration as she joins you on the roof ledge, by being absolutely stark bollock naked and smoking a cigarette. Even though you have neighbours who can see everything you do, and the woodland in front of your house is full of wolves and raccoons staring at you and wondering why a naked man is sitting around, letting the mountain air cool his bits and pieces.

Sex-having has been an integral part of the movies since as far back as my parents (and, unfortunately, my grandparents) or I dare to remember, and I don't see it changing anytime soon. Sometimes you will find a director trying to push the boundaries of what is and isn't acceptable on screen. 9 Songs (2004), the Michael Winterbottom movie, for example, caused an outrage because the actors were actually having sex. The sex-having may have been real, but it didn't make the film any less boring. It also features the most depressing cum shot I've ever seen – and it's not often you get to say that about a movie. So maybe we should celebrate sex-havers in bad movies, we should unite in their clumsy coitus and their doomed booty calls, and accept their blood-filled, gory death scenes. If you look at it in a glass-half-full kind of a way, at least their untimely demise means they no longer have to be a party to whatever ridiculous movie they are starring in.

8
Oh, Hi, *The Room*

For those worried about the absence of *The Room* (2003) from the best-of-the-worst chapter, you'll be relieved to see that it has an entire chapter dedicated solely to its mad brilliance. The reason for giving *The Room* its very own chapter is that it has had more of an effect on the bad film community than any other, and continues to do so. From its confusing obsession with spoons and bridges to its brilliant disregard of self-awareness; the film is so packed full of breathtakingly bad scenes, puzzling plot points and nonsensical dialogue that it really does deserves a chapter all of its own.

Just as people remember where they were the day Elvis died, or when JFK was shot, or when *EastEnders* want from two to four nights a week, those of us in the business of bad movies can remember exactly where we were the first time we saw *The Room*. For me, it was at the end of an uneventful dinner at a friend's house. As we sat in idle chatter with stomachs full of homemade goodness, the conversation turned to bad movies (as it often does when I am in a room). I was enthusiastically regaling a small group of partygoers with an account of the Groundhog Day repetition of the same four shots used in the truck sex-having scene in *Raptor* (2001) when the host suddenly became very animated. 'Have you seen *The Room*?' he asked, to which I replied that, no, I hadn't seen it but I would put it on the list of films to watch if he recommended it. 'No, you can't put it on a list,' he replied. 'You have to see it as soon as you can. It will change your life.' It all seemed a little dramatic, but I do get this level of enthusiasm chucked my way all of the time. Bad-film fans always assume that their favourite bad movie is the best. From *Terror in the Mall* (1998) to *Zombie Strippers* (2008), they always have the title that can be comfortably called the perfect bad movie; which, if nothing else, highlights just how the tastes and preferred criteria of individual bad-film fans can differ. Before I had the chance to reply to the host, he ran out of the room, returning moments later with the DVD. 'You can borrow it, but you need to give it back.' It's not often that a bad-film fan will trust you with one of their movies, especially a prized one, so I nodded and went to take it, only to have it snatched back from me. 'I mean it,' he said, in a tone far too serious for a simple DVD loan transaction. 'You need to give this back to me as soon as you have seen it.' He finally let go of the film and watched as I placed it in my bag, as if he was judging me. I honestly felt that if I hadn't taken the requisite degree of care, he would have snuck into my bag and taken it back again at some point during the evening, deeming me unworthy.

The following afternoon, after many texts from the host, I sat down and watched the movie. Then I watched it again, and then I watched it a third time to make sure that the last two times I hadn't been dreaming or had some stranger come into my flat and spike my drink, because nothing seemed real any more. I instantly loved the film in the same way you would love something that's ugly but has sentimental value; an ornament, a painting, a third child etc. I am ashamed to say that I even thought about not returning the DVD. But after watching it eight or eleven more times, I did eventually return it to my friend, and then we watched it together, excitedly discussing the story and pointing out things like a couple of lunatics.

As a bit of background for any of you who have never seen or heard of the film, *The Room* is what many consider to be an expensive vanity project by the writer, director, producer, actor and melted Howard Stern lookalike, Tommy Wiseau. It has been reported that the film cost somewhere in the region of $6 million to make, and the source of that funding remains a point of intrigue, with many people believing that Wiseau bankrolled the project himself. When you see the quality of the film, you might wonder what they used the other £5,899,999.05 on, and my guess is, it was on a lorry full of drugs and alcohol to help the cast and crew get through the filming. When the film was released in the theatres – to be specific, when it was released in one LA theatre – it is believed to have grossed a box office of just under $2,000. For any normal filmmaker, that low return would have been a blow to the confidence and an extinguisher of hope in terms of a successful career in the film industry. But the vision of writer, director, producer, possible backer and Fabio's hair stunt-double Tommy Wiseau transcended the normalcy of what we mere mortals might define as 'success'. He knew he had something special, and thanks to his determination, his bad-movie-making skills and the burgeoning culture of audiences beginning to crave exceptional levels of movie badness, *The Room* went on to become one of the biggest cult hits of the 21st Century, and it doesn't look as if anything is going to knock it off its pedestal any time soon.

When writing about bad movies, many people have used *The Room* as a predictably lazy journalistic shortcut; but if you've seen it, then you will be aware that that 'bad cinema' doesn't even come close to describing it. *The Room* transcends bad cinema, it even transcends *good* bad cinema. Again, using the binary opposites theory of how bad films become good, the journey *The Room* takes is more of a spiral. It starts, as most films do, in a 'benefit of the doubt' position of 'good cinema', then it travels down to 'bad cinema', before passing through 'so bad it's good cinema', making its way back around to 'bad cinema', then trundling back over to 'so bad it's good', before taking a detour via 'bad cinema' to a new Dante-like position at the bottom of the spiral, which I like to call the 'What the fuck?' level. We are not dealing with any ordinary bad movie here; we are dealing with a mutant.

It is abundantly clear that Tommy Wiseau went out of his way to read all of the rules of screenwriting and filmmaking, and then burned the books in favour of doing things his way. Ryan Finnigan, writer of *The Room: A Definitive Guide*, told me:

'*The Room* breaks every single rule of filmmaking in 100 minutes ... It's indescribable, it's dense, it's unlike anything else you will ever see, and it's an experience. *The Room* should be on every film fan's bucket list.' He is right. I have never seen anything like *The Room* before, and I doubt I will again. Not even Wiseau's subsequent project *The Neighbors* (2015), a sitcom featuring Wiseau in a number of badly-fitting wigs, has come anywhere close to the success of his specular flop. From the very first viewing, bad-film fan or not, you get a real sense that the alchemy Wiseau has created can never be replicated. While in both wilful and accidental bad movies we expect the acting to be wooden and the plot to be either overly complicated or annoyingly simple, *The Room* seems able to ratchet up the levels of crapness to a higher plane of existence. Forget about taking things to eleven, *The Room* takes them to twelve, possibly even to twelve point five.

There are characters who pop in and out of scenes and never get introduced or have their presence clarified; and in some cases characters magically appear in the middle of a scene without any explanation and act as though they've been there the entire time. The plot has many points that, in a normal film, would constitute subplots, but here they are more like narrative *cul-de-sacs*. For example, Lisa (Juliette Danielle) has a delightful mother who casually announces in the middle of a conversation, 'I got the results of the test back – I definitely have breast cancer.' You don't expect a character just to chip that out during a conversation about cakes and boyfriends. In that small scene alone, you will find the nucleus of Wiseau's incompetence as both a writer and a director. No build up, no subtlety, no signs on the actress's face of an internal struggle as she tries to find the right words to use to tell her daughter she has a terrible illness. It's a sudden yet blasé announcement that is crowbarred in and then forgotten about. Literally forgotten about and never mentioned again. *Never.* I wonder what Wiseau was thinking when he wrote it? Did he throw it in to try to make the audience warm more to Lisa? To highlight the precious nature of life? Or was it to fill a couple of minutes with drama, only to run out of time before the story could be resolved properly? If only the writer, director, cinematographer, actor, driver and police photo-fit of a serial cat-strangler was willing to answer any questions about himself or *The Room* without resorting to annoyingly decipherable riddles, I could find out. It is hard to get any sense out of Wiseau. In interviews, he is incomprehensible. His accent and slurred speech make it impossible to keep track of his conversation, and his reluctance to talk about his background or himself is ... well ... just weird. But people love him for it, so why should he change?

The film is peppered with random images of spoons, a recurring shot of the same bridge, scenes of football-tossing on the world's smallest roof garden, and a barrage of confusing dialogue, the delivery of which is hindered by Wiseau's aforementioned thick accent. The origin of said accent is as tricky to place as his verb conjugation. Settling somewhere between Germany and Kazakhstan, this oddly-inflected speech pattern is as hypnotic as it is impenetrable. The mystery of where Wiseau was born and where he grew up is one of the strangest surrounding the film and its director, producer, writer, musical accompanist and *House of Wax* background actor. My friend Adam Spiegelman, television producer and creator of the bad-film podcast *Proudly Resents*, told me about the time he attended a question-and-answer session with Wiseau before a screening of *The Room*: 'Before the movie, Tommy fielded questions. The audience was excited and rowdy. Tommy handled them like a substitute teacher on his first day in class. The questions were from film students asking Tommy why he did something stupid and then laughing about it. Tommy didn't really have an answer. That didn't seemed to bother him. He only got upset when this birthday boy's wife asked him where he was from, and he scolded her for asking such a rude question.'

I experienced a similar thing at a screening in New York. Somebody in the audience yelled out, 'Where are you from?' Wiseau's answer was, 'America. I live America, and don't be so personal.' He stood there shaking his head, as if dismayed and disgusted that such a question should be asked in a public space. His expression was, I imagine, the same face a mother would make after reading her teenage son's internet history: one of disgust and disappointment. Whether this is a ploy to keep us interested or whether Tommy has a dark and mysterious past that he wants to keep on the down-low, I don't know. But it's just another intriguing cog in the ever strange machine that makes up Wiseau.

The plot of *The Room* is basic, as most bad-movie plots are. Johnny (Wiseau) is a successful banker who lives in a small house in San Francisco with Lisa (the same one with the mother who has casual breast cancer), who is his girlfriend. At the start of the film, Wiseau is at pains to let the audience know that Johnny and Lisa are madly in love. He does this by going, almost immediately, into a sex-having scene. In fact, the two of them spend a large chunk of time sex-having. But you should be warned, these sex-having scenes are not for the fainthearted. It's not that they are overly graphic or deviant; there is just something about them that is disturbing on a spiritual or esoteric level. The couple's bed seems to be made of marshmallows and net curtains, as they roll about the place getting into odd positions between and, unfortunately, on top of the sheets.

The texture and pale hue of Wiseau's mottled skin against Danielle's slight tan and odd nipples creates uncomfortable viewing. Remembering the scene now is making me feel a little sick to my stomach, but also making me crave beef jerky and a Tunnock's Teacake. When we showed *The Room* at the Barbican Centre with writers Graham Linehan, Peter Serafinowicz and Robert Popper as special guests, it was the sex-having scenes that got the most horrified shrieks from the audience. But the best reaction came from Serafinowicz who, after watching Wiseau's naked sex antics for a few moments, quietly said, 'Jesus Christ, he looks like a boiled horse.' And when you see the film again, you realise that – *yes!* – that is exactly what he looks like. A shaved, boiled horse. The only let-up our eyes get from this piercing, writhing atrocity is the soft focus and net curtains, which even then offer us only partial blessed blurred relief. However, the relief is always shorted-lived, as the camera cuts to Wiseau's awkwardly thrusting and clenching ass undulating like two lumps of playdough on an oscillation platform.

Despite all the rumpypumpy and lavish gifts, Lisa is unhappy and decides to shpadoinkle Johnny's best friend, Mark (Greg Sestero). Cue more sex-having scenes; although luckily for our eyes, these aren't so disturbing. Lisa then starts talking smack to her friends and family, and anybody else that will listen to her, bad-mouthing Johnny; even confiding in them that he hit her and that he is a bad provider. This accusation is pivotal, as it is the catalyst for one of the most famous scenes and most quoted lines from the film, where Johnny tries to clear his name and convince his friends that Lisa is making it all up, that he's not a wife-beater. Never have the words 'I did not hit her! It's not true! It's bullshit! I did not hit her!' been delivered with so much misplaced emotion and in such an impenetrably strong East European accent. This emotion, much like everything else in the film, is short-lived, and dissipates instantly when Johnny's friend enters the room, leading Wiseau to utter the other infamous line, 'Oh, hi, Mark.'

To try to explain all the ins and outs of what happens in the rest of *The Room* would take too many words, and I'd probably need a couple of flow charts and at least three Venn diagrams. But just to gloss quickly over the finer points, there is an annoying neighbour called Denny (Phillip Haldiman), whom Johnny and Lisa support financially for reasons that (surprise, surprise) are never explained and who dabbles in having a drug habit for all of three-and-a-half minutes; a florist who is so wooden that she could blend in easily with most of her stock; a telephone bug that is supposed to be discreet but that's bigger than the actual telephone; and a rooftop fight scene that puts anything choreographed in *Undefeatable* (1993) to shame. The whole movie culminates in the most depressing-looking birthday party ever, when, in an act of revenge, Johnny plays intimate phone calls between Lisa and Mark where they talk about their affair. Lisa is shocked. Mark is shocked. The rest of the party are shocked, even though you wouldn't be able to tell from their stone faces. What is clear is that Johnny has had enough and embarks on an angry mission of demolition. After he has destroyed half of the living-room and then most of the apartment, the guests shuffle out and the party is well and truly over. Poor Johnny, left alone and cuckolded, has no choice but to grab a gun and kill himself. I guess it's true; they shoot boiled horses, don't they?

Although I had seen *The Room* countless times on DVD and played it as part of the Bad Film Club, it was not until 2011 that I watched it in a cinema and experienced the interactive nature of its audience's response to it. While on an editorial trip to New York, I saw that *The Room* was playing its regular monthly slot at the Ziegfeld movie theatre (soon, sadly, to be shutting its doors for good), with a Q&A session beforehand with Wiseau himself. I snapped up a few tickets, cajoled some friends who had never heard of the film to join me, and bought an American football and a few plastic spoons to take to the screening. The Q&A was confusing. Tommy didn't seem to know where he was for most of it, but he judged a red dress and tuxedo competition, threw around an American football and spoke some garbled nonsense too closely into a microphone. It didn't matter, though. I was in New York, sat in a lovely 1960s cinema with over a thousand fans of bad movies (fans, at least, of *this* bad movie), and I felt at home. The warming browns and deep reds of the old cinema added a lovely glow to Wiseau's usually pasty, tapioca-textured skin, making him look less like a boiled horse and more like a grilled one. So what if he was unsure about where he was or who he was talking to? Who cares that he kept looking off to the two guys on stage to check if either of them knew what was going on? I was in the same room as Tommy Wiseau, and this was going to be awesome.

The first fifty minutes of the film certainly were awesome. It was like being in the audience for *The Rocky Horror Picture Show* (1975), with the entire crowd all knowing what to shout and when to shout it. But here, instead of toast, they threw spoons;

instead of firing water pistols they tossed a ball around; and instead of men wearing heels and stockings, they dressed like drunk pirates. Tommy had presumably left the building by the time the film started, so we were free to laugh and yell as much as we wanted, and it really did create a great atmosphere. Unfortunately, the screening started at midnight, which meant that a large percentage of the revellers were already drunk way before they got to the movie theatre. Common sense dictates that drunk people at a cinema where they encourage heckling, although at times entertaining, will inevitably lead to trouble. It takes only one drunk person inadvertently to say something stupid for the whole atmosphere suddenly to change.

To put you in mind of the cinema layout, the Ziegfeld Theatre has a huge sweeping stalls section that holds about 830 people, and then a slightly raised section behind it that holds about 300. My band of merry, internationally-sourced friends (American, Australian and British) were clumped together at the end of a row about ten from the back. Around us sat a mishmash of college students, young film fans, a couple of guys around our age, and a few three-quarter-length-short-wearing skater boys. We were kind of separated from the rest of the audience, inasmuch as the row in front of us was empty apart from three couples nearer the centre aisle, then there was us, a smattering of more college students, and then the rest of the rows to the back were unoccupied. Being a bad-film lover means I will always choose seats near the back of the cinema on the aisle, just in case I need to make a swift escape (see the chapter on 'How to Safely Watch a Bad Movie'). The fact that we were sat near the back also meant that the rest of the audience couldn't really hear us, and our dark corner position meant that we weren't that visible either. We can thank this fortuitous piece of seat-locating for the ensuing fracas not having turned into a full-blown riot.

As I mentioned, a lot of people had been drinking, and that was never truer than of the camp gay guy sitting in the row behind us, just off to the left. He and his two very drunk girlfriends were enjoying shouting at the screen. Most of the time they didn't know what they were shouting, and the other times they were just mooing into the darkness, but they were young and having fun, so our row telepathically agreed just to let it go and leave them to it. At a bit of a lull in the action, our drunk dude decided he was going to pipe up about how bad he thought the movie was. 'This is a terrible film,' he slurred, and we all agreed. One of the guys in our row even turned, chuckling, and said to him, 'I know, dude, that's why we're here.' DrunkyMcYellypants wobbled and shook his head in disgust, as if he couldn't quite process this, and then he just carried on yelling. 'Fucking hell, this is so stupid,' he quipped, his head now lolling about camply on his shoulders. When that didn't get a reaction, he went a bit further and yelled out, 'Jesus! This is stupid. This is the stupidest film. This is garbage. My eight-year-old brother could do better than this. This is worse than anything I've ever seen. This film is even worse than 9/11.' If you can capture the surprise of reading that statement and translate it into an audible gasp followed by a rumble of anger, you would be somewhere near the reaction of the people in our dark corner upon hearing that nugget of drunken idiocy. I can't think of an appropriate time in any situation within a public space where it would be okay to yell out a sentence that compares a bad film with the atrocities of the 11 September 2001 terrorist attacks. But what I can do is think of the worst time and situation where a person can yell out that sentence, and that would be inside a dark movie theatre full of drunk and patriotic Americans, in New York City!

I would hope that I don't have to explain to you that most Americans are a bit jumpy about the topic of 9/11, but New Yorkers are especially so, and with good reason. They don't mess around when it comes to the topic, and they certainly don't suffer fools gladly, or quietly. The first in our cinema enclave to take offence was the skater boy on our row, who turned in his seat and yelled in the drunk heckler's face, 'What the fuck did you just say, bro? I'll knock you the fuck out, faggot.' The word 'faggot' set off one of the drunk heckler's girlfriends, who leapt to his defence and started screaming,

'Leave him alone! He's gay and he's from Wisconsin.' I'm not sure which part of that was supposed to excuse the ill-judged comment; the gay part or the Wisconsin part, or maybe the combination of the two. I don't know much about American culture. Maybe being born gay in Wisconsin creates some genetic recession that mutates homosexuality into dumbassery. Either way, her explanation did nothing to calm the row. Next to join the fray were a couple of meaty college students, who dived at the heckler from the row behind and held him in a painful-looking headlock. Drunk heckler's friend number two then went into full Pterodactyl screechy drunk girl mode and started punching at the heads of the college boys and screaming at them, 'I will fuck you up, I will fuck you up, I'm from Jamaica, son, I'm gonna fuck you up. Bend over and I'll fuck yo' ass with a motherfucking strap-on.' By Jamaica I assumed she meant the area in Manhattan called Jamaica and not the country. A territory known for its laid-back approach to life probably wouldn't advocate a sex crime in a cinema. How do you get from 'This is my friend who said a dumb thing' to 'I'm going to fuck you up the ass with a strap-on'? And she didn't clarify whether she actually had the strap-on to hand or whether he would have to wait until she either went all the way home to retrieve one or went to a shop to buy a new one. And who is going to hang around to wait for that? As the kerfuffle continued, the American contingent of our group wanted to get involved, the Australians wanted to watch, and we British members sat and continued watching the film, pretending that nothing was happening. As every trip on public transport has taught us how to do.

It was difficult for me, because the majority of the fighting was taking place during another of Wiseau's signature sex-having scenes, so I wasn't sure where to put myself. If I looked at the fight I might become embroiled in it; if I looked at the floor, chances were I would see some kind of rodent or insect, which would certainly be crawling amongst the food debris in this old cinema (if I can't see it, then it doesn't exist); and if I looked up, I would be faced with Wiseau's cramping playdough buttocks. I was onto a loser wherever I positioned my head. The disagreement started to turn into a full-blown fight, with more audience-members piling into the action. A slew of ushers came streaming down to break things up. They grabbed the drunken heckler and the guy who had in him in a headlock, ready to remove the offending parties from the venue. An older guy who was sat a few seats from us calmly shuffled his way to one of the ushers and suggested that the drunk heckler and his friends be taken out first and perhaps put into a cab, because he didn't think they stood much of a chance outside in the wilds of NYC. Plus, if they went out together, the fight would just continue outside the venue, which would attract more attention and police. Offending parties removed, we were all safe to continue enjoying (if that is the right word) the movie. Thankfully, the experience didn't do anything to shake my love of the film; it just sucked me further into the crazy world of Wiseau and his ever crazier fans.

Regardless of Wiseau's performance and penchant for uncomfortable sex-having scenes, *The Room* has managed to garner an astounding cult following around the world, and is held up as the ultimate genre-breaking movie. But is it a movie that exists solely for entertainment, or could it be considered art? It is certainly crazy and unique enough to be considered an accidental comedy, but could it be argued that it also transcends into postmodernist art? In the era of Banksy-style guerrilla street art and internet ambiguity, Tommy Wiseau could be fooling us all, just like Joaquin Phoenix did when he made the documentary *I'm Still Here* (2010) with Casey Affleck, where he pretended he was quitting acting to start a career as a rapper. Those badly-shot, convoluted, non-resolving plotlines could be an artistic choice, and those actors could actually be giving flawless performances as wooden amateurs who can't enunciate or convey emotion. After all, who said that films have to make sense? Maybe mainstream audiences are missing the genius of Wiseau, and he has actually made a scathing satire about the monotony of contemporary paint-by-numbers cinema?

David Lynch once said, 'I don't think that people accept the fact that life doesn't make sense. I think it makes people terribly uncomfortable.' That sums up The Room perfectly: it makes no sense, and it always makes me feel uncomfortable. Don't get me wrong, I love the movie, but even I have to admit to finding some of it too difficult to watch. You can also compare *The Room* to another movie that people said made no sense and made them feel uncomfortable, but went on to gain cult status with university students and film fans: Lynch's own *Eraserhead* (1977). Here is a film that gives no clear idea of where the narrative might be going, includes strings and strings of characters with stories that are never resolved, and makes absolutely no sense at all. I often use *Eraserhead* to scare my students whenever they moan at me for not showing them enough movies. Their cries for less theory and more film-watching are oddly muted once they have seen the bleeding chicken and the radiator woman. What I'm saying is that Tommy Wiseau might just be the next David Lynch. Alternatively, Wiseau really could be just a deluded wannabe filmmaker who landed in LA with the goal of creating a film that would get him noticed. Even though it might not have been for the reasons he expected, and whether it is art or just wonderfully bad cinema, he has certainly managed to do that.

Part of me wishes that he would stop making, or trying to make, more content, because I don't think anything he makes could come close to topping the perfect nature of his first *good* bad movie. But, who knows, maybe one day I'll be writing about how awesome the sequel is. And, as bad-film lovers know, there can be only one title for the sequel: *The Room 2: Electric Boogaloo*.

9
Bad Movie Bad Guys

The bad-movie world certainly is littered with over-the-top, pantomime-quality bad guys. From evil scientists striving for the recognition that has been denied them for so many years, to military men hell-bent on world domination, to just plain old psychotic nut-jobs seeking revenge for all the times they were bullied or rejected or yelled at by a teacher or parent or strangers in the street. Make no mistake, it takes a lot to be an effective bad guy in a bad movie. Your surroundings are already a screaming cliché, and you are fighting against the distraction of a low-quality production, so, unlike a bad guy in a good movie, you've really got to ramp up your performance to be seen and heard above the rest of the crap emanating from the screen.

The good guys have the advantage of being able to take their clothes off to get the audience's attention. No matter how bad a film is, a collection of freshly-oiled and tanned abs as our hero works out in the gym, or a pair of bouncing boobs as our damsel tries to run away from her pursuer, is going to help perk up at least 50% of the people at the cinema. As bad guys are usually character actors, or chosen to play a part because of their quirky looks, people aren't that interested in seeing them naked. Not many people are going to pay to see Gary Busey or Danny Trejo re-enact the dancing in underpants scene from *Risky Business* (1983). If their faces look like that, Lord knows what their personal down below area is going to look like.

The bad-movie bad guy, or girl, has first got to perfect the sneer. For many audiences watching a really bad movie, this visual clue is necessary to signal that the character is, in fact, the bad guy. Sometimes the acting and storyline alone aren't enough to confirm this. There is nothing subtle about the bad-movie bad guy sneer, either. It has to be over-the-top; more like an Elvis impersonator with a fish-hook pulling his lip. If the actor doesn't make it big, the audience just isn't going to notice.

But sneering alone isn't going to cement the bad-movie bad guy into the role of antagonist in the minds of the audience. It has to be accompanied by some impressive eyebrow acting. Eyebrow acting is the stalwart technique of the bad actor's repertoire. I've seen entire scenes where the only real acting is happening in the top third of a character's face. A raise of the right eyebrow to evoke menace; a raise of the left to signal pure evil; both raised at the same time to signal a yawn being stifled. But be warned, once you start to notice how enthusiastic a particular actor's eyebrows can be, you may never watch one of their films in the same way again. You will be constantly focused on those bouncy, hairy lines of distraction like caterpillars doing the Macarena.

The bad-movie bad guy voice also has to be distinct, and needs to settle in somewhere between Dr Claw from *Inspector Gadget* and the guy who does the voiceovers for movie trailers. Low and slow is the most effective. The stalled delivery gives the illusion that the bad guy is contemplating his plan, when in truth the actor is simply trying to remember his lines or to read them off a prop. Blackheart (Wes Bentley) in *Ghost Rider* (2007) is a good example of this.

There is another way to play a bad-movie bad guy, and that's to be completely ineffectual. This requires a level of bad acting that is seldom seen, but of which there are examples, such as air marshal Gene Carson (Peter Sarsgaard) in Robert Schwentke's *Flightplan* (2005), who behaves like a wet blanket for most of the movie. This kind of bad-movie bad guy dictates that the actor should mumble his way through the action so that the audience can never quite understand what he is saying. It also helps if he has an impenetrably thick accent that nobody can quite place, and a face that displays all the jeopardy of a beanbag chair. If you can find all of those qualities in one bad-movie bad guy, then you've got yourself the 'surprise bad guy'. The surprise is twofold: the audience are surprised because they weren't aware that the movie had a bad guy, and they are also surprised because the casting director has picked such an unsuitable actor to play the part in the first place.

Being a bad-movie bad guy is becoming a lost art. In many bad movies, you'd be hard pressed actually to find a bad guy. They are slowly becoming an endangered species. Professional screenwriters with a track-record of quality understand that a narrative needs a crisis and an antagonist to give it purpose and momentum. The bad-movie screenwriter tends to focus on cramming as much action into the film as possible, so that there is very little time for real crisis – apart from the one the audience go through as they decide whether to stick with it or cut their losses and go home early. In focusing on the car chases and gunfights, bad-movie screenwriters tend to forget that their protagonists need something to fight against. The audience also need to have somebody to get behind, to root for and to clearly identify as the movie's hero, and this becomes difficult when there is no benchmark against which the main protagonist can be compared.

It can also be difficult when the bad-movie bad guys are mutant killer animals gone rogue, or intelligent animals gone rogue, or intelligent mutant animals gone rogue, or robots gone rogue, or anything other than a human gone rogue. This is why killers such as these are usually accompanied by a bad scientist or a bad engineer. Without that added human element, it is too difficult for an audience to glean any motive behind the attacks by such creatures. In *Deep Blue Sea* (1999), for example, the sharks aren't just pissed off because they're swimming about in a tiny pool of water, and they're not just seeking revenge for all the times they've had experiments performed on them. If that was the case, they could have easily destroyed the base or leapt out and chomped a few biologists in half at any time – a fate suffered here by corporate executive Russell Franklin (Samuel L Jackson) in one of the best-timed death scenes in movie history. As Tom Scoggins (Michael Rapaport) says during the film, in reference to Dr Susan McAlester (Saffron Burrows), 'She screwed with the sharks, and now the sharks, they're screwing with us.' The sharks are toying with our heroes, making them suffer, but we need a human villain – in this case, McAlester – to translate that to the audience, who will otherwise be left wondering why the sharks are attacking in the first place. Regardless of the production qualities of a movie, an audience will always need the peace of mind that comes with knowing that there is a specific reason for a mutant uprising or an animal attack, and that it's not something that could actually happen to them. If you don't give your audience a reason, they can have no real resolution, and they will leave the cinema unsatisfied. Then you're swimming around in *Jaws 3-D* (1983) territory, and you know what happened to those guys.

Out of all of the bad-movie bad guys, there are a few notables whose performances have been so over-the-top and so perfectly exaggerated that they totally steal every scene they are in. I mentioned my number one favourite bad-movie bad guy at the start of the book, and that is William Forsythe's character Shaye from Dean Semler's *Firestorm* (1998). With his sneering leathery face and threateningly creepy demeanour, Shaye cannot be held behind bars at the Wyoming State Penitentiary any longer; he has to get out and retrieve his $37 million, all of which he will probably then blow on hookers and guns or hookers with guns; I'm not judging, but he is a total badass. The Wyoming State Penitentiary runs a useful 'work in the community' programme for its most trusted and short-stay inmates, whereby they are deployed to join fire-fighters and help extinguish forest fires. But Shaye knows he has no hope of getting on that programme; he can't be trusted, he's just too damned evil, and even though he's wearing the worst-looking, most ill-fitting wig that Wyoming has to offer, he's still exuding a foreboding sense of terror.

Shaye has hatched a plan to get himself on that bus, along with a few hand-picked fellow convicts who will be helpful in getting him to his money in return for a share of it. His ultimate plan to escape to freedom is to kill the prison librarian, a trustee convict who is always chosen for work placements outside; then after the killing, Shaye will start the process of disguising himself as the dead man. Luckily for him, when prisons allow convicts out on a day release to do community work, the only checks they perform are to see that they are wearing glasses and have a tattoo behind their ear. No other forms of identification needed, and no team looking for a missing prisoner in the building. Result! If you've ever wondered what the planned escape scene from *Con Air* (1997) would look like if it were set on a bus rather than a plane, then this is the film for you. Not that Forsythe could ever hope to match the grotesque bad-movie bad guy acting of John Malkovich as Cyrus 'The Virus' Grissom, plus that movie has the balancing benefit of Nicholas Cage to prevent every scene being stolen by the bad guy.

As Shaye leads his band of merry convicts through the blazing forest to their freedom, his behaviour as the archetypal bad-movie bad guy is as perfect as you can get. He is unpredictable, his voice is low and gruff, and his conversations have a 65% threat content. Not only is he willing to kill his enemies, he's not that fussed about killing his own cohorts either, and he spends the next hour picking off his criminal helpers one by one. At one point, he is chagrined that his kidnap victim Jennifer (Suzy Amis) is failing to thank him for shooting dead the gang member who was harbouring lust-filled thoughts about her. Women, huh, they are *never* satisfied.

Best of all is the weird decision-taking by Shaye to put on a fake Canadian accent as a disguise, to transform his identity from dangerous criminal to hapless Canadian fire-fighter – because you can't be scared of a Canadian, they're all far too polite. You may not instantly recognise the accent, but Shaye handily announces to our hero Jesse (Howie Long) that Canada is where he and his associates are all from. It sounds a bit like an American accent mixed with a Venezuelan accent for most of the time. That is, until the scene where they scramble to the outpost out of the smoke, and Shaye yells after Jesse, 'Hey, when we get ooowt of heeere, I'm gooonna buy yooo a nice cooold Canaaadian beer, eh.' The line itself is stupid, and offers nothing more than to reinforce to the audience that, yes, he is trying to be Canadian; but the look that comes at the end of it is brilliant: Forsythe manages to express the murderous intent of his character along with a feeling of disappointment at his own bad acting ability. Every muscle in his face, not just the eyebrows, is working to keep his character to the forefront and his true feelings about the script to the background.

What makes Shaye the ultimate bad guy is his refusal to just die. At the movie's climax, he is punched, shot and hit in the leg with a plank of wood, but remains undaunted. When he tries to escape a fast-moving blaze in a tiny boat, our hero Jesse appears from the water and throws an axe in his chest, causing him to fall overboard. We presume that he must either have drowned or bled to death (what with the bullet wounds and leg injuries); but when Jesse and Jennifer battle for their lives, trapped in the eye of the fire and struggling to keep the oxygen in an upside-down boat, their problems are exacerbated by a gunshot from the water, and we see that it's been fired by Shaye. Somehow, he's been swimming along just fine, firing his gun and not worrying about the hole in his leg or the other broken leg, or the cavity where his chest once was. He's even got the energy for a bit of an underwater gun tussle – these being so much more exciting than dull out-in-the-open gunfights, where you can move about quickly and hide behind objects.

Another shot is fired, and our hero Jesse sinks to the bottom of the drink. Or does he? It's all part of the orchestration of Shaye's ultimate death, which is brilliantly conceived. Thinking that our hero has been shot dead, Shaye appears in the boat to finish Jennifer off; but what he hasn't bargained on is that Jesse sank to the bottom of the lake only in order to gain a strong upwards trajectory. Jesse swims, full force, at Shaye, and forces him upwards so that his head goes through the large bullet-hole he created in the boat earlier. This kills two birds with one stone. The hole is blocked, which prevents the oxygen being sucked out of the boat, and our bad-movie bad guy is definitely dead this time, because his head has been turned into a birthday candle. When the dead Shaye falls back down, head suitably melted, the special effects people have gone that extra mile in their attention to detail. This means that we see the lump of a torso with the tiniest crispy shrunken head on its shoulders plop back into the water. A fittingly diabolical end to a black-hearted diabolical man.

There is no doubting Shaye's inherent evilness, but if it's over-the-top, psycho-crazy bad guys you're after, then the film you're looking for is *Undefeatable* (1993), and the man you are looking for is Stingray, played by Don Niam. If you think the character's name is ambiguous and you are looking for a brief synopsis of the film, the guys at IMDB have summed it up perfectly in just a few words that are both startling and intriguing and almost succeed in making the film appear tantalising – 'Kristi Jones (Cynthia Rothrock) avenges her sister's death at the hands of a crazed martial arts rapist.' Everything you need to know about this film is right there. The bad guy is not just a crazed martial arts killer, and not just a crazed rapist, but a crazed martial arts killer rapist. I don't know if there is such a thing as a sane martial arts rapist, and I don't know if the martial arts part adds or detracts from the evilness of a rapist. Either way, I'm watching this film.

Hand on heart, I don't want anybody to take what I am about to write the wrong way. Of course murder and rape are some heavy-duty topics that have no real place being discussed, seriously, in a book about rubbish films. But, don't quote me out of context, Stingray performs one of the oddest rape scenes I have seen in any movie. As his girlfriend/victim screams, both of them are perfectly still – or their bodies are perfectly still, I should say, because Stingray is indulging in some uncomfortable-looking fervent neck-kissing. The director, Godfrey Ho, then makes an interesting creative choice: he constructs a montage of a steak cooking in a pan, Stingray's head jerking about like a giant chicken, and images of a boxing match on a loop. The scene ends with Stingray taking the half-cooked steak out of the pan and snarfing it down his evil gullet as his girlfriend sits on the floor. If it wasn't for the synopsis spelling it out, I wouldn't have been 100% sure about what had just happened.

You can sense from *Undefeatable*'s opening few scenes that Stingray, with his diabolical mullet hairdo and his black singlet top, is going to be a great bad-movie bad guy. He stands out so conspicuously amongst the bad and continuously high-kicking action. He even likes to collect and keep all of the eyeballs he's gouged out of his victims. Even if you haven't seen the entire film, there is a chance that you might have seen its ultimate fight scene on YouTube, under the title 'Best fight scene of all time' – and the title doesn't lie. In this scene, our psychopath Stingray has gotten himself a knife, but his opponent has only his street smarts and his kung fu skills. Both are trained fighters, but Stingray has the edge, because he's properly crazy. Even his eyes are independently crazy from the rest of him. To prove his craziness, he even starts the fight by licking the blood off his ostentatious Crocodile Dundee-style knife. Dirty boy. He won't be acting so tough when he gets Ebola and his pancreas is shooting out of his asshole.

The sweaty, naked torso fight scene (they both rip off their shirts like the Hulk to help them really get into it) lasts about five minutes and, in that time, Stingray demonstrates how a crazy man fights, with a series of fast punches, kicks and attempted eye-gouges that, to the untrained eye, looks a lot like two actors practising the 'You go, then I'll go. You punch me as I stand here, and then I'll kick you a few times in the stomach as you stand there' method of stage fighting. There are some painfully funny shots. There are times when it appears as though the slow-motion punches are not actually slow-motion at all, but the actors just pretending, and fighting really slowly, the way kids do in the playground. It's a relentless few minutes of fight, punch, kick, kick, punch, kick, kick, kick, punch. But it's all over when Kristi joins in with her mad martial arts skills, and through a series of cool manoeuvres, irony steps in and Stingray's head is smashed into a wall – a wall that just happens to have a protruding nail on it, causing him to gouge his own eye out. It hurts, sure, but he can keep going. He's like the knights that say Ni from *Monty Python and the Holy Grail* (1975): he can still kick your ass, it's only a flesh wound. Eventually, though, our crazed bad-movie bad guy must be defeated (despite what the title tells you), and he is hoist on his own petard – well, he is hoisted up on a forklift truck, by a hook that is jammed into the hole where his eye used to be – dangling and dead, and no longer a threat to women or optometrists.

Not all bad-movie bad guys have to be demented killers; they can be brilliant minds, or desperate men (or women). *The Mutations* (1974) offers an audience double value for money, because it effectively has two bad guys: the evil scientist Professor Nolter, played by actual proper and real actor Donald Pleasence, and his deformed companion Lynch, played by 'soon to be a time traveller and won't have to do these bloody films anymore' Tom Baker. Nolter looks more like a librarian than a maniacal scientist, and he possesses none of the trademark bad-movie bad guy evil scientist trademarks. No mad hair, in fact not much hair at all, no eye patch, no interesting scars, no crazy personality disorder. He's also devoid of much emotion and has no diabolical plan. His only bad habit, if you can even call it that, is abducting people (young naked woman in particular), taking them to his lab and trying to mix their DNA with that of plants, in order to create a hybrid with the strength and rejuvenating powers of both. It's more a peccadillo than anything else. He wants to help create a better, stronger and more resilient human race, and what's so bad about that? Apart from the legions of dead and discarded human-yucca plant hybrids which are strewn around the city, that is. He may have a calm and academic persona, but it isn't difficult to tell that biologist-gone-rogue Professor Nolter is a bad-movie bad guy, because of the contempt with which he treats his assistant Lynch. There is a definite Dr Frankenstein-and-Igor, master-and-slave, relationship between them. They work in tandem: Lynch stalks and abducts the victims, and Nolter experiments on them.

Lynch is a rare form of bad-movie bad guy, inasmuch as you almost feel sorry for him. He is badly facially disfigured and wears – ironically, bearing in mind Baker's now famous *Doctor Who* image – a hat and a large scarf to hide himself from public view. I do feel sorry for Baker when watching this movie. He was having to act under that fake face make-up for weeks. It's not even possible for him to move his lips, and so he talks through his teeth, like a bad ventriloquist. It also makes him dribble profusely, which is one of the reasons I have trouble watching this movie. Show me as much blood and intestines as you like, I'll be fine; but have a character so much as spit in a movie, and I'm almost moved to vomiting.

Lynch is forced to work with a travelling freak circus, and his only friends are a group of little people, an alligator woman, a man who likes to stick skewers through himself and a bearded lady. Lynch hates them all, and to be fair, they hate him too. One of his only reasons for working for Nolter is the hope that the scientist can cure him of his disfigurements. In one scene, Lynch is invited to have a drink with the gang at a birthday party. They tell him how much they like him and say that he is one of them, but they do this only because they know the contempt he has for the freaks. One of them says the line, 'We accept you, you're one of us' which is an obvious reference to Tod Browning's 1932 movie *Freaks*. So incensed is Lynch to be thought of as one of them, even though he technically is, that he destroys the birthday party, angrily kicking over bottles and standing on plates of cake, his big legs stomping about like those of Godzilla on the rampage in a 1950s Japanese movie. With Lynch's long hair, oddly contorted face and violence toward inanimate objects, I am starting to wonder if Tommy Wiseau conceived his performance in *The Room* after watching this movie.

Later on in the film, Lynch wanders through the red light district looking for some comfort, but as he approaches them, the prostitutes look away, not wanting his custom. Dejected, he wanders the streets until he happens upon a card in a shop window that reads, 'Young model gives dance lessons to strict tempo' – which I believe is sex-having code for, 'You can come over to my place and have sex with me for cash.' He walks up the grimy staircase to the young girl's apartment, and during the bargaining over prices, she knocks off his hat and is shocked by his appearance. However, ever the entrepreneur, she tells him not to be self-conscious, and that if he spends a little extra, she can be 'extra nice' to him. But Lynch isn't after sex, he just wants to pay her to say 'I love you'. The scene is heartbreakingly tender; a rare chance to see the pathetic human side of the character. She does agree to it for an extra quid; but the aggressive way she then unzips the front of her flannelette nightly and briskly walks, tits first, over to him, bellowing out 'I love you,' would certainly be grounds for requesting a refund. The disdain in her voice makes it more of a forty-years-married 'I love you' than a blossoming-first-time 'I love you.' Still. It gives the audience a rarefied chance to connect on an emotional level with this bad-movie bad guy, which is probably why the performance is so memorable.

But, pathetic or not, Lynch has got to die, as has Nolter, for littering up the place with walking trees and talking bush-humans. During an experiment, the front gates of Nolter's house are infiltrated by our visiting American scientist hero Brian Redford (Brad Harris), who scales the walls to try to find out just what the scientist is up to. Lynch intercepts him, and after a brief struggle knocks him out with a large rock. Lynch has every intention of finishing him off (I mean in a killing him way, not a sexy way) but is stopped by one of the bug-eyed freaks he's treated so badly, who jumps up and drives a knife into his back. In a scene that has some genuinely creepy moments, the gang of freaks (I don't know what the collective noun for freaks is ... I've just looked on Google, and apparently it's a gawp of freaks; remember that, it could come in handy during a pub quiz) slowly walk toward him throwing knives, until eventually he stumbles and is turned into fresh food for the guard dogs.

While fiddling about with some science, Nolter fails to notice that one of his experiments-gone-wrong has landed on the glass roof. Down comes the bushman, who overpowers Nolter and envelops him with his killer-plant body, giving Brian a chance to free the victim and flee the building. The mutated bushman is left to perish along with Nolter as the entire house burns to the ground, killing the bad-movie bad guys and all of the evil, evil science.

Cold-hearted science is good, but if it's the ultimate sneering, mumbling, impenetrably-accented bad-movie bad guy you're after, then look no further than *Anaconda* (1997) and Jon Voight – he's won Oscars, you know, for acting. In this movie, Voight is playing Paul Serone, a greasy snake hunter who pretends that his boat is in distress just so he can get a lift up the Amazon and poach himself a giant killer snake. Once his real identity is found out, he spends most of his time sitting on an old boat giving the evil eye to Terri (Jennifer Lopez) and Danny (Ice Cube). He encapsulates all the traits that an over-the-top movie villain should posses. Mumbling speech, check; shuffley walk that will vanish later when he needs to win a fight, check; massive scar on his face from having been bitten by a snake, check; crazy, twitchy eyes, check; and the ability to say great lines of badly-written dialogue like, 'This river can kill you in a thousand ways,' check.

His effectiveness as an all-intimidating bad guy is only somewhat hindered by the odd accent Voight has chosen to give Serone. It's kind of halfway between Mexican and Russian, with a little West African thrown in. You can become distracted by it if you try to place its geography, so you may miss some of the action if you don't concentrate. However, from the way he prepares dinner – chopping, scaling and bashing the fish like he is a WWE competitor – you know that, no matter what Generic-stan accent he has, if he treats people like he treats his food, they are all in danger. He's a tough guy, a real man who can get out of any situation and fuck you up. Even when tied to a post and threatened with a knife, he manages to jump up and trap and kill poor skittish Denise Kalberg (Kari Wuhrer) with just his legs. It is never made clear whether her cause of death is his powerful leg muscles crushing her windpipe, or whether the close proximity of her head to the crotch of a man who hasn't changed his trousers or underpants in weeks simply overpowers her senses, causing her body to give up and shut down. Serone is also made entirely of sneer; but I suppose, as an actor, you have to do all you can in your performance if you're going to try to be noticed alongside Jennifer Lopez's ass.

The genius of Serone is that, much like Lynch, he is very difficult to kill, and actually gets to have not one death scene but two. When he finds himself outsmarted by Terri and Danny (not something that happens very often, I'm guessing), he comes face to face with the giant anaconda he's spent all of the film chasing. Unfortunately for him, he doesn't get to add this snake to his trophy collection, as it slowly crushes him to death and then eats him whole. The filmmakers could have stuck with a CGI snake for this scene, but they added in a little animatronic puppet fun with a 'gullet cam' shot in which the audience get to see Serone's grisly death from the point of view of the snake's throat. It's like that scene in *Little Shop of Horrors* (1986) where Steve Martin's dentist character gives a root canal treatment to a giant mouth, but instead of teeth there are glistening and pulsating slabs of snake muscle. It must have been difficult for Voight to act inside a massive meaty condom, but he does so with faultless dignity.

Death number one out of the way, it's on to death number two. The snake is now out of its constraints and, even though it is full of Serone, hurtles after Terri. No doubt about it, Jay-Lo looks way more appetising than lumpy Jon Voight. Tragically, like so many body-conscious divas before her, the anaconda obviously feels that she will be judged if she snarfs down two humans (I blame all the photoshopped snakes in those glossy magazines), so she vomits Voight out before she goes after the girl from the block. Out slides Voight, even lumpier than before, covered in snake juice and with a face like a bag of ping-pong balls. It takes skills to keep up the bad-movie bad guy persona after a snake has just spat you out, but still Serone manages to keep his cool. He doesn't shriek in pain, he doesn't have much of an expression at all, and we assume that he's dead – until, that is, he looks up at Terri and winks at her before falling to the ground and finally expiring. He actually takes the time and effort to wink at her! Proving that not even being slowly digested by a giant snake can cramp his style.

Being the sinister asshole can take many forms in bad movies, and the rich, snooty and evil traits of Brad Wesley (Ben Gazzara), the antagonist in *Road House* (1989), are a perfect balance for the stronger and holier-than-thou personality of protagonist Dalton (Patrick Swayze). The film is as testosterone-fuelled as it could possibly be, with bar fights, martial arts bust-ups and a scene where Dalton, casually perching on a table, sews up his injured arm in front of a full-length mirror. This means that here, the bad guy needs to be even more prominent than usual; not in a crazed amateur dramatic way, but in a wonderfully bonkers spiteful and malevolent way.

We first see villainous Brad Wesley as he descends on his home in a helicopter, dressed like an evil Man from Del Monte, flying close to Dalton in a flagrant game of my-one-is-bigger-than-your-one. The only thing that could make the scene any better would be if there was a hilariously clichéd hillbilly landlord standing next to Dalton, wearing denim dungarees and complaining that the flying machine has spooked his horses. Luckily, that is *exactly* who is standing next to him. Farm-owner and OAP Dexy's Midnight Runners tribute-band member then exclaims, 'I swear he does that just to piss me off' – and he would be right. Because that is how petty Wesley is. Nothing is as passive-aggressive and yet dripping with wealth-bragging bravado as a man parking his helicopter in his driveway and flying it too close to his poor neighbour's livelihood while, unironically, wearing a panama hat. His next act of wilful malice is to hold a large party in his garden, way past bedtime on a school night. *A school night.* I know what you're thinking; how could he possibly get any worse? Surely once you've seen a large, uncoordinated, hairy white guy dancing about with no top on, there's nowhere else to go. Well, you'd be wrong. Later in the film, we see his flagrant disregard for the Highway Code as he weaves his car across both lanes while driving home. Even though there are no other cars on the road, and technically he's not putting anybody in danger, he's still being evil, because he's not going to let a bunch of white lines tell him where he can drive his car. Maverick.

Like other ridiculous bad-movie bad guys in any number of action scripts seemingly written by teenage boys in their bedroom at night, Wesley has henchmen. You would imagine a man with his own helicopter, mansion and a collection of very expensive tea cups would be able to afford the best of the best – ex-CIA, bounty hunters or even members of the secret service. No. What he does have, however, are a bunch of clueless dumbasses, one of whom is so fat that his stomach hangs with some startling fury over the waistband of his jeans, which are 'kept up' with braces. Wesley keeps this shower of buffoons in line with regular punches to the face, Miss Piggy-style karate chops and knees to the balls. I wonder what their Christmas bonus is? A gentle slap on the neck, perhaps? Brainless henchmen aside, he does have Jimmy (Marshall R Teague), the kick-boxing badass who is destined to become Dalton's nemesis. Although Jimmy is tough, he could never make it to real bad-movie bad guy status, because all he has are his moves. Even when he tries to smack talk, it never comes out right. During a fight with Dalton, he confusingly says, 'I used to fuck guys like you in prison.' What does he mean by that? And how is Dalton supposed to react to it? Is it a mistake? Was the line, 'I used to fuck over guys like you in prison,' but nobody noticed until the edit? Obviously it ends up badly for Jimmy; later, in a fight with Dalton, he has his neck gouged out and is left floating down the river. It's what he would have wanted.

As with all bad guys, Wesley must meet his demise, and the shoot-out at his mansion mixes a high body- and blood-count with hilarity, as FatbellyMcBraces avoids being shot in the face only to be bested by a giant stuffed polar bear that falls and traps him under its fury heftiness. Wesley cares not for fat men trapped under polar bears and is sticking to his assholery to the very end, mocking Dalton as they play a game of hide-and-go-shoot-me around the house. Wesley talks about how he killed Dalton's best friend – calling it a 'mercy killing' – and he stands and delivers his well-thought-out, well-structured and well-enunciated bad-movie bad guy speech about how evil he is and how he's probably just going to kill everybody Dalton has ever loved, because he's so evil and that's what evil people do. But it's hard to feel threatened by anything he is saying, because the fat guy is still under the giant stuffed bear and is wriggling about behind him. Speech over, and the fight is on. It's *mano a mano*, Dalton versus Wesley, in the taxidermy room, which contains just the one small white sofa conveniently placed for Wesley to fall over it. No matter how many spears he throws, and how much compassion Dalton shows by not ripping his throat out when he is clearly bested, Wesley is bound by the bad-guy code to play dirty, and so reaches for his concealed gun. Luckily, all of the town's businessmen have just turned up *en masse* to take a shot at him, and they literally blow him to bloody pieces. Again, though, his tough-guy death is marred by the flailing fat guy who is still trapped under the dead polar bear.

It should be remembered that the bad-movie bad guy is your friend, your saviour even. He or she is the one who is going to keep your interest as the film limps on – the one with all the best lines, the best facial expressions and the best wardrobe, and the one who gets to shoot at the annoying hero. Without their terrible, over-the-top, hammy acting, bad movies would be dreary and lifeless and boring as hell.

10
I ♥ Mockbusters:
Snakes in the Air
Or on the Ground?

In 2006, in a shabby cinema in central London, Joe and I sat watching the David R Ellis film *Snakes on a Plane*. We had been sent to the screening by a newspaper that wanted to interview us straight afterwards, probably to capture the giddy euphoria we were certain to experience when met with Samuel L Jackson yelling about getting motherfucking snakes off motherfucking planes. Surely, it would be a home run. Bad-film-lovers watching a highly-anticipated bad movie + too many Maltesers = emotive editorial piece. The problem was, we both found the film a little dull.

When the internet hypes up a product as much as it did *Snakes on a Plane*, especially when there is a big Hollywood name attached, it becomes difficult for it to live up to all of the expectation. It was this expectation that prevented the movie, in our eyes, from achieving a so-bad-it's-good status. It was too self-aware, it was too tongue-in-cheek, and we were expecting too much from it. As I have mentioned before, the intentionally bad can never be as good as the unintentionally bad; you lose the exhilaration of discovering a *good* bad classic. What made the experience even more disappointing was that the film had already been out for a couple of weeks, so any aspect of it that could have contained surprises was already well and truly spoiled.

The reporter met us outside the cinema, all teeth and no hair, and ushered us into a dingy members-only bar around the corner, where he spent an hour trying to cajole some kind of positive review out of us. After he'd gone, we spent a further hour exploring the place and posing in ridiculous positions next to the various oil paintings that were dotted around. When they inevitably threw us out, we ventured into a sunny London to peruse any and all second-hand DVD shops we could find. As I don't live in London anymore, I constantly tell myself that when I do visit, I will look at the historical buildings, ride the London Eye and visit the museums, but I always end up in second-hand book stores, or in Croydon.

As the two of us shuffled with the rest of the human traffic through the city, we spied our next target, a scruffy-looking shop with two large bins of VHS tapes outside that promised us a world of bad-movie wonders. We peered in from the doorway, spied the bulging floor-to-ceiling DVD stock and took in the familiar second-hand-video-store smell, which is a heady mixture of damp carpets, bad body odour and Gregg's pasties. It was our favourite kind of second-hand store, the kind with no organisation, no alphabetisation and a 'just put it over there on that pile, Steve'-style filing system.

Ten minutes and six copies of *Hawk the Slayer* later, I was beginning to worry that I wouldn't find anything interesting, until my eye was caught by a small pile of DVDs near the door. These were different. The covers seemed shinier and smoother, devoid of sticky glue residue – a known side-effect of bad-movie covers, a result of being labelled with dozens of decreasing price stickers. The shelf they were near had the word 'Imports' printed on a yellowing rectangle of paper, which was partly obscured by a copy of *Flubber*, and as I plucked one at random from the pile, I was surprised to find that it was a brand spanking new release.

Usually I am not drawn toward shiny new DVDs, but on this occasion, as I had found only one older one worth buying – a copy of Linda Blair's 1979 four-wheeled epic *Roller Boogie* – I started to forage. When I reached the third film in the pile, my excitement could hardly be contained. Not even the price, £12, put me off wanting to buy it. To put this into context, £12 is six or seven times more than I would usually pay for a film. But I just had to have it. I grabbed the film, and clung on to it as tightly as Dean Kane's hold over the Christmas film market, until I found Joe. He was at the back of the shop reading the cover of the MC Hammer biopic *Too Legit* (2001). When I showed him what I'd found, his face contorted into the same expression of joyous exhilaration as mine, and we both eagerly pawed over the title ... *Snakes on a Train* (2006).

Finding *Snakes on a Train* on the same day as having to sit through *Snakes on a Plane* felt like the movie Gods were trying to make it up to us. The reward for our patience was to deliver unto us a truly awful movie, a movie in which the CGI *and* the acting both look as if they were hastily created on the computer of a 14-year-old boy. For those unfamiliar with *Snakes on a Train*, the only similarity it has to its better known cousin, *Snakes on a Plane*, is that they both have a lot of snakes and they rhyme with each other. I think keeping it on a form of transport was a bit of a cop out; I would have gone for *Snakes in Champagne* – a gritty drama where a socialist warrior spikes magnums of champagne at a posh party with killer snakes. Or *Snakes on Elaine* – a romantic comedy where musical theatre actress Elaine Paige must juggle her successful stage musical career with a job as caretaker at a reptile house. In *Snakes on a Plane*, the snakes are there to prevent a man from testifying in court. *Snakes on a Train*, however, is about a woman who keeps vomiting snakes into a jar, and she just so happens to be on a train. It has no big Hollywood stars, no insane internet hyperbole, hardly any budget, is claustrophobically filmed – for the most part in one setting, on a 'moving' train – and the first six minutes are in a foreign language with no subtitles, so you're never quite sure what's going on. But this wonderfully strange, badly-lit, cash-in movie was my first experience of the mockbuster, and it fostered a long-standing love affair with the movies of American production company The Asylum.

For those not familiar with mockbuster movies, these are films designed to ride the publicity coattails of the bigger

Hollywood smash hits; they usually head straight for the DVD market, ideally to be released *just* before the movies they are mocking. Smaller, independent production companies trying to profit off the success of specific big screen movies with similar content isn't a new thing – hey, *E.T.*, *Mac and Me* is calling you, and it's holding a tiny alien that looks like a sex toy. It is The Asylum, however, that has become synonymous with the practice, a practice that is growing in popularity by bringing audiences notoriously low-quality sound-alike versions of big summer hits. If you couldn't wait to see *Transformers* (2007) on the big screen, no problem, how about *Transmorphers* (2007)? It might have a score of only 1.7 on IMDB, but you won't have to watch Shia LaBeouf eyebrow-act his way out of every scene with fighting robots who sound like spoons going through a washing machine. *Speed Racer* (2008) a little too racy for you? How about *Street Racer* (2008), starring the guy who played a busboy in the popular American soap opera *The Young and the Restless*? Not sure if the remake of *Robocop* (2014) is for you? Then may I present *Android Cop* (2014), a film that touched one of the Bad Film Club audience members so much that he called it, 'shit on a fucking plate'.

My personal recommendation is *Almighty Thor* (2011), and not just for its pound-shop filming budget, but for Richard Grieco's portrayal of Loki. He spends the majority of the film wearing a black boiler suit and looking like Edward Scissorhands with a meth problem.

The joy of mockbusters is not only that they give independents the chance to beat the big Hollywood studios to the punch, but that they have managed to make a real impact on those Hollywood studios. A rational person might laugh at the idea that Hollywood heavyweights could, in any way, be bothered by these underdogs; surely these films should be seen as a mild annoyance rather than a real threat? At most they could be likened to an ant at a picnic, or a gnat at a picnic, or a mouse at a picnic – I guess what I'm saying is, don't go on picnics, they are full of pests and never fun. But getting back to the mockbusters, Hollywood did indeed become super-peeved at the cashing-in of these low-budget mockeries at the expense of their multi-million-pound films. In 2012, Universal Studios slapped The Asylum with a lawsuit for attempting to release the film *American Battleship* (2012), the title of which was deemed too similar to that of the Peter Berg-directed movie *Battleship* (2012), loosely based on the board game of the same name. Although, in my opinion, Berg's movie is not much better than the mockbuster now retitled *American Warships* (2012). The Asylum's offering has a formulaic, clichéd story, amateur-grade actors and a dull execution, and so does Universal's – only Universal spent way more money, so who is the real loser there?

Universal is far from being the only big player to have been shaken by The Asylum's business model of the straight-to-DVD schlockmockbuster. Later in the same year, MGM, Warner Brothers and New Line Cinema all took umbrage at the apparent advantage these low-budget producers were taking of their big-budget titles and publicity to draw audiences to their cheaper knock-off movies. But should they really be that worried? Is anybody going to buy *Transmorphers* mistakenly thinking that they are picking up any of the Michael Bay *Transformers* movies? The cover of the DVD alone should tell any sane person that this might not be the film they are really looking for. Even if the artwork on the front fools you, the movie stills at the back should give you more of a clue. When you see that the movie is full of people you've never heard of, wearing black and running around shonky locations that might very well have been filmed on a 1984 Sony BMC100P Betamax Camcorder, that should be enough to tell you that it's not a multimillion-dollar production. Common sense says the small independent mockbuster is no financial threat to the big summer blockbuster movie. On the other hand, the badly-made mockbuster can be a lot more entertaining.

If you do a side-by-side comparison between *Snakes on a Plane* and *Snakes on a Train*, then *Snakes on a Train* wins hands down. *Snakes on a Plane* was a product of internet infamy, the title and concept being leaked and shared long before the film was finished and distributed. But for all of the excitement, the film was just dull, and probably because it fell foul of its own aspiration to be a bad movie. It became too self-aware, and too aware of the audience and what they might be expecting. The filmmakers had a big-name star and global attention – both of which are suicide for the bad movie that is still in the stages of production. Now the plot *has* to make some kind of sense, now the acting *has* to be at least a little good, now the effects *have* to be passable.

Take the opening of *Snakes on a Plane*: majestic sweeping aerial shots of blue waters, exotic beaches and tanned revellers splashing about and having fun. It's slick, it's evocative and it looks really good. The start of *Snakes on a Train* is pretty much an unvarying shot of a cactus in a desert. At one point you think the camera is going to move, but it doesn't, it just stays on the cactus. *Snakes on a Plane* heightens our expectations, *Snakes on a Train* gives us nothing, and it will continue to give us nothing until the conclusion, when it will give us the satisfaction of a magnificently bat-shit crazy ending and the biggest treat of all ... the end credits.

In *Snakes on a Plane*, the snakes are on the plane because a man named Sean Jones (Nathan Phillips) has witnessed gang leader Eddie Kim (Bryon Lawson) beat a guy to death and is being flown to testify against him. Despite the fact that you can't even get a half-empty bottle of hair conditioner past airport security these days, Kim manages to sneak on a time-release crate of venomous snakes and arranges for his henchmen secretly to spray the passengers with pheromones, thus ensuring they will all get attacked. As plots go, it's pretty out there; but in some ways it's too viable, almost believable, and what use is that to a bad movie? Now *Snakes on a Train*. The reason the snakes are on the train is that a woman in Mexico has been put under a Mayan curse, causing snakes to hatch out of her stomach and escape from her mouth. These snakes are pieces of her and her soul, and so must be kept together so they can be presented to a shaman in LA who will lift the curse. Because, although the curse was put on in Mexico, it can be taken away only in Los Angeles; that's how curses work, it's an international business full of red tape and magic loopholes. Don't ask too many questions. The woman and her boyfriend/partner/snake-catcher are attacked and the snakes get loose, causing havoc to the other passengers, because they are cursed snakes and cursed snakes are the worst kind of snake assholes. There's a curse, magic snakes, even a subplot about organised crime. Is it believable? No way. But that's what makes it such an entertaining bad movie. I could follow *Snakes on a Train* for the entire film; *Snakes on a Plane* lost me within the first 12 minutes.

If ever there was damning evidence that trains are more fun than planes, we need look no further than the respective endings of the two movies. Spoiler alert. *Snakes on a Plane* has the infamous line from Samuel L Jackson's character, 'I have had enough of these motherfucking snakes on this motherfucking plane' – and he certainly speaks for us all. The solution is simple (and one that should have occurred at least an hour and a half earlier): shoot out the windows, depressurise the cabin and watch as the snakes are sucked out of the windows. Fly the plane home, and everybody is happy – apart from the dead passengers, of course, and the family having a nice picnic that is interrupted by falling dead snakes. (I told you, picnics are a nightmare.) Bad-film novices might expect something similar from *Snakes on a Train*. Poor novices, they really don't know how unreasonable bad films can be. After a bit of chanting from the boyfriend/snake-catcher, the poor snake woman takes a turn for the worse and starts to transform into a giant snake. She/it kills the boyfriend/snake-catcher and then throws herself/itself out of the window. Now we've got a giant snake-woman surfing on the train roof, and an inept middle manager trying to hot-wire the train to gain some kind of control. A foreboding darkness envelopes the carriages, and this can mean only one thing: yes, the giant snake-woman is now an even bigger giant snake-woman and is eating the train, for some reason. If the passengers are amazed when they jump from their carriages to witness a mega-snake devouring their train, imagine the feeling of abject confusion they must feel when they see the snake then being sucked up into the sky by a magic tornado before vanishing completely. That has to be a win for the mockbuster bad movie over the pre-planned bad movie, surely?

The mockbuster obviously suffers from a lower budget, along with student-grade actors and the post-production abilities of a tiny monkey, but as far as fun and adventure go, it wins hands down. It's not the cashing-in that the big Hollywood studios should be afraid of, and it isn't the fact that these low-budget endeavours could be stealing focus from their own high-budget movies. It's the spirit, enthusiasm and revelling in the fun of filmmaking that draw movie fans to them. What mockbusters also have over the big studio productions is the ability to take risks with their storylines. Once you've seen one car chase or alien invasion, you've seen them all; but a cursed woman vomiting up tiny snakes into a jar before turning into a train-eating mega-snake, you don't see that every day. Long may they continue.

11
Christmas Movies:
Jingle Bells and Silent Nights

I unashamedly love Christmas. I love the sparkly, tacky ornaments and miles upon miles of static-shock-giving tinsel. I love the pop-up shops that burrow themselves into vacant storefronts and sell goods with faded packaging containing decorations that come, DeLorean-like, straight out of the 1970s. Cash only. I love the atmosphere, the songs, the costumes, the TV shows and, most importantly, the films. Nothing makes me happier than to be sat in front of the television on a freezing cold night, the Christmas tree twinkling in the corner, groaning under the weight of all the baubles, a box of Dairy Milk next to a hot chocolate, and a Christmas movie playing on the telly. Perfect. Every year when flicking through the Radio Times (the *only* time of the year I buy it) I ask myself the same question – just how many times *can* they remake *A Christmas Carol*? There seems to be a version of it for every kind of audience. Would you like your Dickens with Muppets? (I'm not criticising *The Muppet Christmas Carol* (1992), before you reach angrily for my e-mail address; nothing says genius more than Michael Caine acting amongst felt.) Maybe you'd prefer your Dickens performed by a gurning CGI Jim Carrey? Perhaps a musical version? Maybe a version starring Kelsey Grammer from *Frasier*, or one that has a cartoon walrus playing the Ghost of Christmas Yet to Come? One thing we can all agree on is that *Scrooged* (1988) is by far the best adaptation of the story, and that Bill Murray's version of Scrooge is a triumph of contemporary cinema, and we'll leave it at that. I *said*, leave it at that.

This may be viewing the past through egg-nog-coated spectacles (yuck), but it seems that during my childhood and adolescence there would be at least two big-studio Christmas movies a year released in the cinema. Over the past ten or so years, this trend for big-budget seasonal movies looks to have dwindled. Sure, there will always be the classics on the television to fall back on, nestled between the cookery shows and a million different depressing soap specials. Not forgetting Raymond Briggs, who is also there to add some merriment, and then immediately take it away again. Seriously, Raymond, what is with the end of *The Snowman* (1982)? We were all having such a wonderful time flying above the oceans, arsing about with the snowmen and happily getting down at their party. You could have ended it there: kid goes to bed and wakes up on Christmas morning refreshed and full of magic and wonder. But instead you went and made the final thirty seconds play out the most heart-wrenchingly bleak scene of destruction and sadness. Merry Christmas, your new best friend is dead.

Everybody has their favourite Christmas movie; of course they do. My boyfriend loves *National Lampoon's Christmas Vacation* (1989) so much that he went out and bought some of those moose eggnog cups. It's hard to justify spending £80 plus postage on two novelty eggnog cups when there isn't really an eggnog tradition in the UK. We now use them for hot drinks all year round, to make sure we get our money's worth. I watch the same movies every year in the lead-up to Christmas. I have only to catch a glimpse of the opening titles to *It's A Wonderful Life* (1946) and I start bawling like a child. *Home Alone* (1990) and even *Home Alone 2: Lost in New York* (1992) are also favourites and, in my opinion, examples of perfect Christmas movies. Although I should say that all of the scenes in *Home Alone 2* with Brenda Fricker I could live without. I don't care if it is Christmas and I have to suspend my disbelief to enjoy all the 'feels', there is no way a plotline involving a crazy bird lady living illegally and undetected in a room above Carnegie Hall befriending a small child and luring him back to her place isn't supposed to end in a terrible tragedy. Possible Christmas infanticide aside, the first two *Home Alone* films have got everything you need at Christmas: family drama, an interesting story, great bad guys, John Hughes-style snowy festiveness and slapstick comedy. Yes, they can be a little schmaltzy, but what's a tiny bit of schmaltz at Christmas? It serves as a reminder for audiences that people shouldn't be dicks to each other, especially at Christmas, and isn't that what the baby Jesus wants us to think during the festive season? It should also be noted that the other *Home Alone* movies, *Home Alone 3* (1997), *Home Alone 4* (2002) and *Home Alone: The Holiday Heist* (2012) are not being counted here as official *Home Alone* movies. I know this is a book about bad movies, but there are some movies the titles of which should never be uttered aloud. As far as Christmas movies go, they are dead to me.

The period from the very end of the 1980s to the end of the 1990s certainly seems to have been the heyday of the Christmas movie, with big-budget family films attracting large audiences and box office returns, from *Santa Claus the Movie* (1985) to *Jack Frost* (1998) – and by *Jack Frost* I mean the one where loveable Michael Keaton's dead dad character returns as a snowman to hang out with his son, not the one where Scott MacDonald's dead serial killer character comes back as a snowman to seek murderous revenge. Maybe Briggs was right to kill off that snowman; I don't think I trust them.

Post-1999, a switch must have gone off in the heads of movie studio executives, who realised that, actually, people are already full of goodwill at Christmas, and it isn't really necessary to be spending a large chunk of budget on seasonal movies; audiences will go see anything Christmassy, regardless of effort or quality. This, I believe, is how *Deck the Halls* (2006) with Danny DeVito and Matthew Broderick got made.

Deck the Halls has managed a whole 6% rating on the Rotten Tomatoes website. If you have never seen it, all the information you need to know about its comedy content is wrapped up in Danny DeVito's character name, Buddy Hall. You see? Buddy *Hall*. Deck the *Halls*, get it? It's a play on the Christmas carol, and it's his last name, and that is exactly what the film is about, decking the halls. The plot follows two warring neighbours competing to see who can exude the most festive spirit via the medium of Christmas lights and decorations adorning their homes. The strange thing about this movie is that both lead characters seem to be the antagonist, locked in a constant battle of seasonal ass-hattery. They hate each other, they become too focused on their bitter feud, they lose the respect of their family, they realise the true meaning of Christmas, they find brotherly love and common ground, Merry Christmas everybody, thank you for your money, here are some sparkly lights to look at over the credits. It's as if somebody has taken plot points from every single feel-good Christmas movie, thrown them into a spin-dryer and constructed a story around the parts that have become statically attached to each other. The problem is that as soon as the realisation hit Hollywood that putting any word pertaining to 'Christmas' on a product would guarantee an audience, the market was blown wide open for cinematic dross built upon goodwill to all – especially the pumpkin-spiced gullible ones.

Somewhere along the way, the filmmaking community lost its Christmas mojo. These days, most of the Christmas movie releases go straight to DVD or straight to online distributors and cable channels. The quality of the movies thins each year as the audience dwindles. I have no problem, as such, with the lower-quality Christmas movies; the only thing better than a Christmas movie in my house is a really, really bad one. But the lack of *any* good-quality big-budget Christmas movies being released into cinemas could also be having a detrimental effect on moviegoers' expectations. Neglecting the market one year diminishes expectations that there will be a worthwhile Christmas release the following year, and so on, until the Christmas movie becomes dangerously close to being a genre that only my generation will keep as a memory. We will bore our kids, as we settle them down in front of the Jumbolator 4000 HD 1000 inch TV, playing scratchy-quality VHS versions of *Jingle All the Way* (1996). 'I remember when we would watch films at Christmas at the old movie theatres. Every year there would be a funny movie about how to injure criminals, or how to make cynical city folks believe in Santa Claus by singing Christmas songs, or about putting our faith in something that was less preachy than Jesus but you could still call faith.' Maybe Fox News and the conservative media are right; maybe the liberal media are waging a war on the festive season, trying to snuff out the word 'Christmas' altogether, and soon classic films will start being renamed to give them less Christmassy titles: *White December Holiday, It's a Wonderful Time of the Year, Isn't it?* and *Starbucks on 34th Street.* Or maybe it's just that the current trend seems to be making films aimed at a Christmas cinema-going audience rather than at people who want to get that feel-good Christmas spirit from the big screen. The big-budget movies that used to be saved for the Easter break and the summer holidays are now, suddenly, popping up in November and December. *The Hobbit: An Unexpected Journey* (2012), for example, was released on 13 December, and saw kids and adults alike flooding into the cinema with not an elf shoe or candy cane in sight. *Star Wars: The Force Awakens* (2015) was released on 17 December and quickly overtook Santa *and* Jesus to be the most talked-about thing that month. Maybe it's because our other media outlets have become so saturated with sickly Christmas specials that we don't need the cinema to fulfil that role any longer. All you have to do is open up the television listings magazines to read descriptions such as, 'This year the cast of *The Big Bang Theory* will be learning about the true meaning of Christmas and friendship as each is visited by a Ghost of Science Past.' (Note to self: pitch that idea to Warner Brothers, it's pure gold.) Or maybe we don't feel we need to get our pre-packaged spirit from the big screen anymore because there is now more Yuletide goodwill and heart-string-pulling to be found in department store adverts than can be found in the entirety of *Nativity 3: Dude Where's My Donkey?* (2014).

If you are still in the market for some Christmas spirit during the festive season, and you like your Christmas films on the right side of bad, then I can't recommend too highly *Santa's Summer House* (2012) and the mind-boggling *A Bulldog for*

Christmas (2013). If I were to ask you to imagine what you thought the plot to *A Bulldog for Christmas* might be, what would you come up with? Go on, I'll wait here a moment while you think. What kind of Christmas movie plot would suit a film with that title? Did you do it? Let me guess, you probably came up with some plot about a little girl, maybe with a dead mother or living in an orphanage, who makes a wish at Christmas for Santa to deliver to her a bulldog. That's the only dog she's ever wanted. But that nasty stepmother/orphanage owner keeps telling her that Santa isn't real, and that instead of celebrating Christmas, she should keep doing all the housework and being a general dogsbody? Then, one night, Santa arrives with a bulldog and a plan to break her out to her live with him and Mrs Claus in the Candyland Village at the North Pole, and it all ends happily ever after with elves and reindeer eating cake and singing songs. Was it something like that? That's what I thought when I saw the title. How wrong I was. *A Bulldog for Christmas* is actually a film about a surly college student, who looks like a thirty-year-old punk porn star, who is cursed by an elf and turned into a bulldog in order to learn about the meaning of Christmas. Yeah. You're looking like that after only reading a synopsis; imagine the expression you would have on your face after watching the entire movie. I can only assume that the lessons a bulldog learns about Christmas are how to drink from the toilet bowl and shit tinsel onto the floor of the downstairs bathroom, so that when you go to the toilet in the middle of the night your bare feet squish down on sparkly poop. It's a one-location oddity that an actual human wrote and then other humans made. If nothing else, it demonstrates that the straight-to-cable/DVD market is so in need of content that they'll let any ding-dong write a screenplay. It is this message of hope that I pass on to my screenwriting students.

That is not to say that *Santa's Summer House* is any less bizarre. At some point, a small-time film producer must have thought, 'Let's get all of the z-list '90s action stars and put them in a Christmas film together and shoot it in July.' The result is a gluttonous cornucopia of bad acting, with Robert Mitchum's son Christopher playing Father Christmas (or Pop to his friends) and proving categorically that acting talent isn't genetic. I was sat on the sofa with my boyfriend as we flicked through the channels looking for something interesting to watch that morning when we stumbled upon this movie, and it was the best stumble I took that year. We joined the movie about 25 minutes in, and were hooked in by the sight of Cynthia Rothrock's unmoving face trying to emote. Watching the words being pulled out of that face was so hypnotic that we cancelled our plans for later that day so that we could watch the movie again from the start later on. Yes, I could have recorded it, but that would have meant knowing the movie was playing but that I wouldn't get to see it in all of its glory until another four or five hours later. I'm sure my friends will have more children to christen. I regret nothing.

The plot is based on the premise that a group of strangers who are taking a bus to a fancy resort are enveloped by a mystery fog (which the filmmakers don't seem to have had the budget to shoot, because that bit is told by a narrator and never seen) and end up in a summer house owned by two characters named Nana and Pop, who are secretly Mr and Mrs Santa Claus. It's not just the limited story, told so ineptly, that makes me love this 'Christmas' movie – the budget for which, as with *Bram Stoker's Legend of the Mummy 2* (1999), didn't stretch to filming outside the location of the house – it's the obvious slapdash nature of it. What director David DeCoteau has managed to do is make a Christmas film that can be shown in the summertime, separating itself from other obvious Christmas movies and thereby avoiding any competition – apart, or course, from the competition of well-made films available all year round.

Apart from the usual badness found in these half-baked movies, the film also contains a confusing 12-minute scene where they play croquet. 'You're exaggerating. It probably lasts only a few minutes, and you've taken some artistic licence.' No! The whole 'Let's play croquet in the garden for some reason' montage lasts just over 12 minutes; I've timed it. And watching the minutes roll past on my watch was a lot more entertaining. It's clear that the director was banking on the fact that, during these obviously improvised shots, the actors would appear less wooden. Sadly this is not the case. Even though some of them are obviously trying to pretend that they are really enjoying themselves (and that they actually understand how to play croquet), there is only so much croquet an actor can feign interest in and an audience can tolerate. It's like trying to keep up the enthusiasm during a game of Monopoly. Sure, you're all gung-ho at the start, but after a few hours it's hard to maintain the same level of exuberance for rolling a dice and pushing a tiny dog around a piece of cardboard. In this scene, however, it's the cardboard that is playing the game.

Even though it is the height of summer, and even though there doesn't seem to be any reason for it, Ma and Pop decide to have a Christmas celebration, with the added fun of a secret Santa. Unfortunately, because of the mystery fog (which we still can't see), they are all going to have to make their gifts instead of buying them. No, there are no shops nearby. No, there is no internet. No, they don't have their own car. Stop asking questions; you're spoiling it. In the end, it turns out that our Pop is actually the real Father Christmas. Those pictures of all of the guests, which are up in his study, aren't creepy or indicative of a murderous stalker, he's just been watching them because he wants to make them happy. Maybe it's the fog (nope, still haven't seen it) or the wine or the intimate, half-naked Jacuzzi chats, but nobody questions the validity of his claim – even though he has no beard and wears only shorts and Hawaiian shirts. Ultimately the time spent at the house makes everybody appreciate each other's love and friendship, and the gift-giving ceremony reinforces the true meaning of Christmas; it's the thought that counts, and if that thought is half a pad of paper, a USB stick from a teenage boy that you *hope* has been wiped of all pornographic material, or a picture of your face enduring a croquet marathon, then you should be grateful.

Contemporary Christmas schlock is fine if you're after a happy ever after, but if you're looking for a bad Christmas movie that is unnerving and unsettling, then the festive horror movie is steadily gaining in popularity. After all, nothing says happy holidays quite like a knife through the clavicle, or a sociopath with an elf fetish. There are almost as many Christmas bloodbath movies as there are family favourites – *Black Christmas* (2006), *Silent Night, Deadly Night* (1984) and *Santa's Slay* (2005) to name but a few. One of my favourite seasonal horrors is *Christmas Evil* (1980), which also goes under the titles *You Better Watch Out* and *Terror in Toyland*. It centres around Harry (Brandon Maggart), who grows up a little damaged and Christmas-obsessed after sneaking downstairs on Christmas eve to find Santa in the living room, on his knees, with his face full of his mother's vagina. (The kid's mother, that is; Santa with a face full of *his* mother's vagina would be weird.) You can't really blame the kid for being a little affected after witnessing such a scene; it affected me too, because it gave me flashbacks to a pornographic Christmas film I was once given called *The Tits that Saved XXXmas* (2003). No matter how hilarious the title, nobody should subject an elf to that kind of working environment. It's not sanitary, and it's also a health and safety nightmare: far too many slip hazards in one place.

As a grown up, Harry has covered his apartment in Santa- and Christmas-themed objects, cut-outs and toys, and to further cement his obsession with the jolly old fat man, he even works in a toy factory. He's full of the joys of Christmas giving; but, unfortunately, he's the sort of guy others take advantage of, and he also gets a bit twitchy when his co-workers bitch and moan about working around the holidays. So when Harry discovers that he's been duped into covering a shift as a favour for a supposedly sick colleague, whom he then sees out drinking in a bar, Santa's little helper goes into full angry-elf-montage mode. Humming a creepy Christmas tune, he makes himself up a Santa suit, turns his battered old van into a sweet ride with the inclusion of a painted-on sleigh, and gets out his bumper book of naughty and nice children to help fulfil his calling as the most shuddersome Father Christmas known to the North Pole. The sinister music, low lighting and pot full of scissors within easy reach as he reads from his children-who-annoy-me book do nothing to help negate the psycho Santa vibe. The whole *mise-en-scene* lets you know that this fat man is contemplating punishments a little harsher than a lump of coal in the stocking.

To be fair to the kids on his naughty list, his justifications for some of their entries are a little tenuous. Some of his reasons for singling them out are valid. 'Throws rocks at dogs' – I agree, that's a bad kid. 'Uses profane language' – it's not the end of the world, but if the kid is peppering every sentence with a swear word, maybe he shouldn't get his X-Box. But 'Picks his nose' and 'Negative body hygiene'? Surely that's nearly every kid that has ever lived? You might as well add in, 'Thinks Adam Sandler movies are the funniest things that have ever existed' and 'Finds his/her genitals a pleasurable distraction from life.' As psycho stalker Santa Claus, he's been spending his time spying on children and writing about them in a big book, but now that he's become *actual* Santa Claus, he does at least fulfil his brief and deliver gifts to the good and disadvantaged children at the local hospital. If you want to be picky about it, they are toys he has stolen from his company; but a good deed is a good deed, regardless of where the deed was sourced. It's not all gifts and giggles though – this is *Christmas Evil*, after all – and it doesn't take long for this Santa to snap. He goes full bad Santa when a gaggle of snarky yuppies start making fun of him and his costume. Who wouldn't? '80s yuppies are the worst, with their rolled-up sleeves and slicked-back hair. *Boom!* He goes on full attack using the only arsenal he has to hand, and that sarcastic ballbag Greg gets a toy soldier right in the eye. *Wham!* Foster is taken down by a tiny axe to the head. *Scplooge!* Bradley is the last to fall, and spills his Christmas cheer all over the snowy sidewalk.

Harry spends the rest of the evening killing people and delivering gifts – a post office worker's wet dream – until he is set up by a group of angry torch-carrying villagers; the same kind you'd likely find in the pages of a Mary Shelley book. You don't often get angry fire-carrying mobs in modern-day movies; it's all guns and knives, and not enough sticks and oily rags.

After fleeing to his brother's house for refuge, he is greeted not with milk and cookies but by his brother trying to strangle him. Harry has had enough of everything – and, by this point, the audience have certainly had enough of his brother's acting, which seems to have come from the 'shout every line' school of dramatic arts, so the punch in the face Harry delivers to him comes as a blessed relief to one and all.

Then comes the strange and puzzling ending to the film. Harry is panicked and anxious and needs to get the hell out of there, so he drives his sleigh-mobile angrily through the snow. What's he going to do? Flee to Mexico? Set fire to the children's hospital as payback for the constant bad hygiene and nose-picking? None of the above. What Harry does next is drive the sleigh-mobile through some fencing and then off the side of a bridge – but it doesn't plummet to the bottom, it turns into a Christmas Chitty Chitty Bang Bang. A dishevelled and startled-looking Father Christmas (looking almost as startled as the audience, I presume) flies off into the night sky, across the Moon, as the last lines of 'The Night Before Christmas' are recited. Nobody was expecting that (see chapter on what bad films have taught me), and I'm not sure I understand what it means. Is it suggesting that the real Santa Clause is a knife-wielding maniac, so we should all be good children in case he comes down the chimney with a puppy in one hand and a shiv in the other? Maybe the intention was for this final scene to convey how the mind of *evil* Santa was interpreting his imminent death? If so, this being a bad film, the execution was never going to give it any kind of logic or the audience any satisfaction. What we are presented with is a confusing mishmash of serial killer shocks, genuine Christmas cheer and Disney happy ever after; but it's still loads better than *All I Want for Christmas* (1991).

The horror genre may be one small sector of the industry that is still embracing the Christmas movie tradition, but another now re-emerging one is the evangelical right-wing Christian film. These films are produced and distributed by those who have taken it upon themselves to be the guardians of our seasonal morality by promoting the true meaning of Christmas. This preachiest of all the film genres is gaining some momentum in conservative households, and is being lapped up by lovers of bad movies, due to the quality of the productions and the patronising way in which they try to 'slip in' religious values with all the subtle nuance of a weasel trapped in a drum kit.

The problem with a lot of these church/religious group-sponsored Christian-message movies is that their story arc choices set them up for ridicule. There is nearly always a bad guy who doesn't 'believe' and who mocks the good Christian man who does, but by the end of the action, both will have been lifted into the light of God and learned an important lesson about the meaning of Christmas. Not the expensive presents, office parties and Iceland prawn rings – the *true* meaning, the *Santa's Summer House* meaning and then some.

Take *The Christmas Candle* (2013), for example. This morality sermon is distributed by EchoLight Studios, whose CEO is Republican party politician and God's book club buddy Rick Santorum. If you don't know him, he's the guy who said that contraception was nothing more than a licence for people to have sex for fun instead of for procreation – which is what God says sex is for, in a bed, in the missionary position, while married, to a person of the opposite gender, because, you know, gay people are yucky and stuff. This means you just know the film is going to be fair and open-minded from the start. The plot focuses on Hans Matheson (David Richmond), a progressive preacher sent to Gladbury – yes Gladbury in Englandshire; it's somewhere in the county of Teapotcister; you must have heard of it, because even though it sounds a lot like the sort of place any Radio 4 sketch show would set a parody of a Dickens story, the filmmakers wouldn't just make up a name like that. Gladbury has a tradition; every 25 years an angel visits the local candle-maker and blesses a candle, which will grant the prayers of the person who lights it on Christmas day. It's like a godly version of a Kinder egg. But Matheson causes tension in the village. He is a man who likes light bulbs and wires and all things new, as opposed to the candle-maker who likes, well, making candles, and all holy heck breaks loose when he takes things too far and dares to put electricity in the church. The Devil's fireworks in the house of God? Never! To make matters worse, the magic Jesus candle goes missing, and the whole village is turned upside-down with turmoil. The only positive outcome is that the progressive preacher learns to appreciate the beautiful flicker of a simple candle. Fuck progress, flame is the future.

It sounds like the plot of a quaint Sunday-night BBC drama, or a Sunday-night ITV drama, or a Sunday-night Sky One drama, or a pick-a-channel-they're-all-the-bloody-same-anyway Sunday-night drama. But if you're looking for cosy plotlines and jolly characters, you're out of luck. What you *do* get for two hours is a mixture of characters who bounce from one test of faith to another; invention over tradition, Christianity over faithlessness, chicken over fish. And as if the film wasn't bad enough, with star Sylvester McCoy being out-acted by his sideburns, they plonk poor Susan Boyle into the mix to play the innkeeper's wife. Traditionally innkeepers' wives were supposedly all jolly and rosy, greeting customers with a hearty laugh, not unwelcoming, awkward and wooden, with a face like a bewildered cabbage. Perhaps her character would have been more believable if they had rubbed peanut butter onto her gums and dubbed her voice like they used to do with animals in television commercials. Boyle trying to act her way through a scene amongst professionals only highlights her ineptitude; something that the director must have felt when trying to get her pudding face to settle on any expression other than 'Ehh?'

At least *The Christmas Candle* has a get-out clause of being set in the quaint and filmable past. Sometimes it's easier to avoid noticing the level of badness in a film if the scenery is nice and distracting. If you squint your eyes during *The Christmas Candle*, the screen becomes a moving wallpaper reminiscent of cheap and flimsy Christmas cards depicting cheerful robins and distant snowy rooftops of smoky villages. But when a preachy film is contemporary, it serves only to highlight the worst of it.

Amongst the familiar, there isn't as much to distract you from the action. The best (or worst) example of a modern-day conservative-Christian, atheist-bashing movie has got to be either *Christmas with a Capital C* (2011), directed by Helmut Schleppi (which is an amazing name for a human), or the Razzie-award-winning *Saving Christmas* (2014), starring Kirk Cameron. The only saving grace of the first one is that it's got a Baldwin brother and some semblance of a story. *Saving Christmas* is just a succession of dull conversations in a car between Cameron's character and his brother-in-law, who is losing his faith in the holiday while wearing a really bad jumper.

Christmas with a Capital C serves to remind us how bad atheists really are: we must remember that they are terrible people with no heart and no feelings, and all they want to do is go around replacing 'Merry Christmas' with 'Happy Holidays' or 'Season's Greetings'. This is a conservative shorthand warning to the audience that those terrible liberals are threatening Christmas, and all that it and Christ stand for. The world would be a better place if it wasn't for them pesky kids who want to lump Christmas in with other festivals and celebrations happening around November/December (Hanukkah, Kwanza, Festivus etc). As far as the characters in *Christmas with a Capital C* are concerned, the 'Happy Holidays' moniker is a modern-day scourge, cutting the Christian purity of Christmas with secular talcum-powder filler. You could try explaining that the song 'Happy Holiday' was written way back in 1942, and that you've been getting Christmas cards that say 'Season's Greetings' since the 1970s, but they're not listening to that, they're on the internet watching Kirk Cameron hailing the banana as proof of the Lord's existence. (That's out there; look it up.)

This 'killing Christmas' plot is at the heart of *Christmas with a Capital C*. Our antagonist atheist Mitch Bright (Daniel Baldwin), who was the old high-school rival to the now Mayor Dan Reed (Ted McGinley), swans into town and immediately tries to change years of tradition. He's moving back and is hell-bent on snuffing out their Christmas celebrations with the news that, sorry, God doesn't exist and, by the way, get that nativity scene down from outside the municipal building, your kid can't sing carols in the town square, and you all need to read up on the separation of church and state. He's an atheist, you see. He's petty, and empty inside. He can tell a child right to her face that she can't sing her festive songs next to the Christmas tree in the town square. Her cries echo inside his empty heart like a pebble bouncing down the Grand Canyon. He also beefs up his dickishness by running for Mayor on the promise of less God, more business, or something to that effect.

If this were just a story of these two warring small-town characters, it might have opened up a valid debate on the issue of boundaries around religious celebration and the validity of gracing public spaces and government-owned property with Christian-specific artefacts. However, the film also stars Brad Stine, playing Ted's best buddy Greg Reed, and here is where it crosses over from interesting ideological discourse into right-wing, whack-a-mole liberal-bashing territory. If you don't know who Brad Stine is, he's a conservative Christian comedian who looks like a '70s catalogue model in a bad wig. He put out a comedy album called *Put a Helmet On* (2003) and a comedy special that was filmed in Virginia because, according to him, that State represents traditional America – or, as he puts it, 'Thomas Jefferson America'. I'm sure you get all you need to get about the values of this performer from that information.

The script has superimposed Stine's stand-up routine onto the film's dialogue to create pockets of protest in which he espouses his views on keeping the Christ in Christmas. He spends his time telling the townsfolk that Americans are going to lose their country if Christians stop saying 'Merry Christmas', because it is, after all, Christmas with a capital C, and if you don't like it, his advice is to 'put a helmet on'. The scenes with Stine are the most painful parts of the film – apart from the bit where we are surprised to see a full-grown stuffed bear in the Mayor's office and the diabetes-inducing family scenes with McGinley. Stine's monologues bang on about how atheists and non-Christians are diluting his faith and that Christmas is the hardest to stomach. At one point, he even stands on a chair in the middle of a diner to re-enact his 'It's not "Happy Holidays", it's "Merry Christmas"' routine. Once you've watched Kirk Cameron talk about God and bananas, maybe you could look this up as well. Seeing is believing, and all that.

As the local populace start to turn against him and his sidekick, poor Mayor Dan becomes obsessed with winning the war against Mitch and what he is doing to his beloved Alaskan town. Dan's wife, who dishes out advice between baking cookies and being the perfect Stepford wife, reminds Dan that they are Christians, so instead of fighting Mitch they should pray for him – something his daughter has already suggested, after popping over to offer Mitch some Christmas cookies, only to find a dark and empty house. Turns out, Mitch isn't such a bigshot after all. His house is empty because he isn't moving back to retire, he's moving back because he's broke, miserable and alone. In fact, to reinforce how solitary and depressing it is not believing in a God, at the end of the film he's in the dark with a candle, because he can't afford the lighting. If he had a saviour, he'd be a lot happier. And that is, ultimately, what happens. The townsfolk trundle over to his house on Christmas Eve after church with candles and food and hymns and the milk of human kindness. At last, Mitch sees the light! All it takes to change a person's belief system is some sausage rolls and chorus of 'Come All Ye Faithful'. Christians aren't bad people and atheists really *can* be saved. It's a Christmas miracle.

For all of its moralising and judgemental criticism of non-Christians, *Christmas with a Capital C* does have a saving grace, and that is the title song – called, of course, 'Christmas with a Capital C'. It's by a Christian group called Go Fish, and is one of the best examples of white middle-class sampling and mum rapping you will find. Kicking off with Stein's 'Happy Holidays' rant, it pretty much goes through the issues of the film, culminating in a catchy chorus, 'It's called Christmas, what more can I say? It's about the birth of Christ, and they can't take that away. You can call it something else, but that's not what it will be. It's called Christmas with a capital C.' If you can't stomach the whole film (and not many people can), at least listen to the song. But be careful: it's catchy, really, really catchy.

It would seem that the focus of many Christmas films – new, old, high-budget or no-budget, Santa or Jesus – is to make us all think about and appreciate each other, our friends and our families around the holidays. *Jingle All the Way* (1996) has as its moral centre the message that consumerism is bad and makes us crazy, so always remember the true meaning of the holiday season until consumerism consumes us and we end up becoming the very thing we are trying to consume, because that is the only way our children will love us. *Santa Claus Conquers the Martians* (1964) reminds us that just because your children live on another planet, that doesn't mean they can't have gifts and a Christmas tree. It also lets children know that they too can have nightmares into their late sixties, having been trapped in a room on a spaceship with a creepy fat guy for hours. And *Elves* (1989) tell us that just because somebody works for Father Christmas, that doesn't mean they won't stab you in the penis.

Part of me wishes that Christmas movies would make a comeback as an important part of the festive celebrations, like they were when I was a child, with their big budgets and big schmaltzy storylines. But another part of me rather enjoys the fact that independent cinema is taking over where the big studios have left off. A new breed of 'have-a-go filmmakers' are bringing us their version of what Christmas means, and it is, for the most part, wonderfully terrible. If I have to get my holiday spirit from bulldogs, washed-up action stars and begrudged Christians, then I'm happy. Even a bad Christmas movie is still a Christmas movie, and that's good enough for me.

Conclusion:
How to Make your Own
Bad Movie

You made it to the last chapter; and, most importantly, I made it to the last chapter. Nobody could have seen that coming. I've done my best to show you some of my favourite bad movies, bad guys, studios and genres, and I hope there have been a few titles discussed in the preceding pages that you would consider getting on DVD or watching on Netflix, or however people are consuming their films these days. (How are you watching then in the future? Are they beamed into your mind?)

Whereas the bad movies of the past will always be with us, the future is more uncertain. At this moment in time, there is a slew of wilful bad movies, low-budget creature-features, overly-loud action movies and delusional vanity projects to appease everybody, but the bubble has to burst at some point. Made-for-TV 'bad on purpose' movies are in danger of becoming a novelty item, and you know what happens to novelty gifts at Christmas: you play with them for a bit, and then they end up in the recycling or the charity shop or the bin.

I believe that as long as there are fans of cinema who are willing to try something different, and big Hollywood studios who are more interested in investing in explosions than in paying attention to narrative and production, there will always be bad movies of some form being made; and most of them will find their way into my ever-growing collection.

But just in case any of the readers of this little book are bad-movie torch-carriers of the future, I've put together a simple step-by-step guide on how to make your very own bad movie, so that between us we can make sure that our brand of movies doesn't become extinct. With this in mind, I present your ultimate guide on how to deliver a substandard and critically-ridiculed cinema experience that, one day, may become a cult classic. You'll hopefully find this a helpful companion on your quest to disappoint audiences, not just in your own country but all over the world. In the following pages, I will be covering all of the aspects of filmmaking you will need to screw up in order to achieve the most effective cinematic failure. Didn't go to film school? Not a problem. Haven't had the time to hone your filmmaking skills from the bottom up? Don't worry about it. You don't need any knowledge of the practicalities or theories of cinema to make a shitty movie. Never even made it through a DVD director's commentary? Relax. Nobody has. Listening to the thoughts of other directors isn't important; in fact, I'd go so far as to say that having actually watched a movie at any time in the past will be more of a hindrance than a help to you.

Cameras ready? Then let's start making bad movies!

We'll begin with what many filmmakers consider the most important part of production, the idea. Your idea can be inspired by real events – a quiet conversation on a train between a young daughter and her father, for instance, or an argument in a restaurant between two exhausted lovers, or a true story of bravery in the face of adversity by a local hero. These are all very well if you want to win awards and critical acclaim, but we're not in the business of audience satisfaction, we're here to make a bad movie. With this in mind, try to make your idea either as obvious or as simplistic as possible; something that never keeps your audience guessing, with plot twists any toddler or OAP could spot. Alternatively, you could try to make it as needlessly complicated as possible; if you can't bore your audience into submission, maybe you can befuddle them into it. Remember, you have around an hour and a half of screen time to fill, and how you do that is exceedingly important. As a bad-film maker, you need to decide if you are going to go for creating a sense of agonising frustration within your audience, so that they begin praying for something, anything, interesting to happen, before they attempt to hang themselves with their Twizzlers or asphyxiate themselves with a mouthful of Maltesers. Another option is to fill your hour and a half with exposition-heavy dialogue, five or six pointless subplots, and meaningless technical jargon you got from Wikipedia, used out of context and incorrectly. Both are acceptable as separate strategies; put them together and you may actually bend time.

Whichever path you choose, you should always remember that many other films have been made before yours – and when I say many, I mean quite a few, more than 150. This means that many film ideas can be viewed as unoriginal and derivative. For example, there is boy meets girl, girl likes boy, boy isn't sure, girl seems nice but has a crazy friend/family/annoying dog/demanding job, boy and girl settle down and get married. This is already the narrative foundation for many big-budget studio movies, and audiences could be growing tired of being fed the same thing over and over again, but with different posters. But over at the bad-movie camp we say, if it ain't broke, don't fix it. The reason that the big Hollywood players keep churning out movies that are variations on the same theme isn't that they are lazy and money-orientated, it's that people like those films, and people aren't stupid. Would a stupid audience keep Adam Sandler's career going for so long? No, I don't think so. So why would you want to swim against the tide? Grab your filmmaking trunks and swim with it, embrace it, and your film is sure to be just as bad as a major studio production. If it worked for Tommy Wiseau, it can work for you too.

Many writers protect their screenplays from copyright infringement by registering them with the Screen Guild of America, and protect themselves from being sued by taking out errors and omissions insurance (also known as professional liability insurance). But thankfully your idea will be so terrible that not even the most desperate of film graduates will be tempted to sneak it and claim it as their own; and, with any luck, your actors and crew will be so new and blinded by the excitement of being on a 'film' set that they are unlikely to sue you for property damage or personal injury. Now you've got your million pence idea, it's time to move on to the next stage; development and financing.

To develop and finance your idea into an actual movie you're going to have to be confident; but that shouldn't be a problem. The directors responsible for some of the worst movies I've ever seen have been very confident people – some might say overly so – but that's not a negative thing when you're looking to finance a romantic alien space comedy. Inflate and embellish your idea, then tell it to as many people as possible. Bother producers when they're out having lunch with their families. Constantly call production companies. You should also try going to as many development events at film festivals as you can and, while there, corner any meek or mild-mannered guest speakers, or people who have less important jobs on film productions, and tell them about your idea. Make sure to talk as manically and energetically as you can. Rant so much that you spit canapés or alcohol in their faces as you talk, and remember to get really passionate when you start describing the space station tentacle sex scene. Producers, directors and movie studios are very busy most of the time, so giving them a little extra work by constantly demanding their attention isn't going to make much of a difference to their schedules, and they could probably do with talking to people about new and fresh ideas. Ultimately they will welcome your tenacity – even though the restraining orders or physical violence you receive may make you think otherwise.

It is also important to note that when entering into correspondence with said producers, directors or movie studios, you should try to be as arrogant or as passive-aggressive as possible. Pretend that you've already got big-name Hollywood stars involved, that Tarantino has already agreed to be your director – but don't let on that he yelled his agreement over his shoulder as he ran to his car to get away from you outside a TGI Friday. You could also mention that there is already Academy Award buzz around your project, even though all you have is the title and a strap line: '*Alien*

Proposal. He's from space, she's from New Jersey, but when the mother-in-law comes to live with them, even the infinite universe isn't large enough.' As long as you sound convincing, nobody will have any reason to question you; but if they do question you, be sure to respond with the disdain this deserves. After all, you shouldn't need to be questioned; you've seen *Citizen Kane* twice, you know what you're talking about.

It takes a lot of time and effort to plan and finance a feature film. Some productions can take years to fund. However, if you follow our slapdash approach to the rules of filmmaking, you should be able to hurry your project through in no time. Don't waste your time with filing cabinets full of forms and mountains of paperwork. Your mind is a steel trap; you have no need of paper. Text messages and late-night Facebook chats are all it will take to secure who and what you need for the next three months, or four, maybe two, we'll play it by ear.

Should it transpire that nobody in Hollywood wants to back the development of your movie, you might have to finance it yourself as a vanity project or from small sums of private investment – perhaps your mate Dave's company could contribute, or you could ask Roy to hand over some of his trust fund. Traditionally, when filmmakers find themselves with a smaller budget, they take their idea and tone it down, lose the big set-pieces and focus on the smaller ones, maybe take a more dialogue-based approach, which is more workable on a modest budget. Do not bother with any of that. Your idea is big, so you must think big. Even though your budget is small, which will make your vision almost impossible to film effectively, you must still try. There are plenty of actors and actresses who are just starting out and who will do your movie for free; and who needs a lot of crew members when you can get Dave and Roy to help out? Don't forget that you've probably got a teenage cousin doing a media studies BTEC who can do you some CGI on his computer in return for nothing more than a couple of sneaky bottles of cheap vodka. The lower the costs, the lower the quality, and that is exactly what we are striving for here. HD may be all the rage in big-name cinemas, but let's not forget that grainy camcorder footage also has its place, and that place is straight-to-DVD or cable television.

If you're lucky, this lack of planning and absence of any discernible eye for detail will ensure that your film stands out as an even bigger travesty. It is also reassuring to know that if you run out of money two-thirds of the way in, you have the option of just halting the production and then carrying on a year or so later, when you have topped up your funding. This will also give your audience the opportunity to play a game of 'spot the changing waistlines and haircuts between scenes'. It will keep them on their toes, and also distract them from the plot. Speaking of the plot, it's time to get it down on paper. Onwards to the writing stage.

Screenplays are the foundations upon which great movies are built, but they are also the marsh-holes that gobble bad films up and drag them down into the swampy darkness to live amongst ill-judged Kevin James sequels and Nicholas Cage projects. And what's wrong with Nicholas Cage movies? I'll tell you what's wrong with them: nothing, that's what. Audiences can't get enough of his oddly morphing face and confusing hairline. And you'd be privileged indeed to lie amongst such grand company. Before actually writing their script, screenwriters will spend a large chunk of time on treatments and character profiles. They know the structure, the A and B plots, and they have their beat sheets and their scene outlines to pinpoint where each nuance of plot and character occurs. They are able to tell you everything about their inner and outer characters, from where they went to school to how many sugars they take in their tea. You, on the other hand, already know your plot. Like I said before, your mind is a steel trap. And as for character biographies, does an audience really need to know where Steve had his first kiss when he's wrestling with a zombie alien mother-in-law? No. No they do not.

Here are the only character profiles you will need to know if you are making a bad movie. The male protagonist has a strong jawline, talks in snappy comebacks and has an intense stare. The female protagonist is standoffish at first, but becomes more friendly toward the end and falls in love with the male protagonist, and has big tits. The friend of the female protagonist is quirky, with funnier lines, and has quite big tits – but make sure they're not as big as the main woman's big tits. The alternative is to have her with no tits and with glasses. The friend of the male protagonist must be annoying and just a tad sexually aggressive. Luckily he will be killed off early in the film. Other characters have no biographies and serve only to move the plot forward through conversation and through being disposable food bags for creatures. They will also be invaluable in their role of informing the main characters of events from the past or in the present that are far too expensive to film. All of these characters should have the ability to get over the death of a close friend or family member within hours, and be ready for sex-having by the end of the day.

When it comes to the presentation of your screenplay, you need to know that most studios and production companies adhere to a strict standardised layout. The easiest way to ensure you get this right is to use either a commercially-available program such as Final Draft or a free one such as Celtx; both of these will put your screenplay in the widely-accepted industry standard, so that you can concentrate on the creative rather than the technical. However, sometimes it can be a little fiddly to download and learn a new bit of software; plus, you don't really trust computers – you only use them for Facebook and Google. Listen to your gut on this one, because if the idea is good enough – and you know that it's the best, so that's not a problem – everyone will see past the fact that you've just centred everything in a Word document and printed each scene on a new page. Once written, e-mail it out as an attachment that no computer program can open, or photocopy handwritten pages and post them out.

When writing for your characters, try to make their dialogue as unnatural and stilted as possible, and also make sure that their reactions to dangerous situations are annoyingly glib. Never forget that your words are the only tools you have with which to create a delicate and colourful narrative, and if you mix all of those beautiful colours together with a few ham-fisted strokes, you'll get yourself a lovely shade of muddy brown. This is the colour of really bad movies. If you recall, earlier I mentioned that audiences love the familiar when they go to see a film. The same thing applies when you're writing your script as it did when you were 'planning' your idea. Try to pepper it with as many clichéd and well-worn lines of dialogue as possible. Go ahead and run the gamut, from, 'You're never going to get away with this,' and 'Cover me, I'm going in,' to, 'I have a bad feeling about this,' and the classic, 'I can explain. This isn't what it looks like.' An example of a line that is both glib and clichéd could be used in a scene where your male protagonist encounters the dead body of an obviously athletic chap with the contents of his chest scattered around the room. Have your protagonist walk casually over to the corpse, put his hands on his hips and say, 'I guess somebody finally found this guy's weakness: [pause for effect] bullets/bombs/knives to the face [delete where applicable]'. Audiences love that stuff, so put as much of it in as you can.

It is also important to remember when writing romantic scenes or sex-having scenes to dispel the notion that you need to treat these with any kind of sensitivity or carefully-expressed intimacy. Bulldoze on in there, making sure the dialogue mimics the sort of corny lines uttered by sweaty men on a Friday night in any inner-city nightclub. If you can't think of any, why not let your actors have a go? Just because they can't act their way out of drama school, that doesn't mean they couldn't be a Noel Coward when it comes to writing. Who can forget the immortal line John Barrowman utters to his co-star in the film *Shark Attack 3* (2002)? Having suffered through an unbelievable (in more ways than one) shark attack that has caused quite a few shocking deaths, our male protagonist turns to his female counterpart and says, 'I'm feeling pretty wired. How about I take you home and eat your pussy?' Improvised by Barrowman as a joke but then kept in by the director, this is not only startling and unnatural-sounding (and I've never met a person for whom that pick-up line was successful), it has the added bonus of seeming like something that might be read aloud by a prosecutor in a court room.

Once the planning and scripting has taken place, the next step might be to storyboard the action in order to map out the significant incidents, the positioning of the actors and the camera angles and movements. Many studios and production companies use professional storyboard artists who will bring your story to life, capturing the minutest of details in your *mise-en-scène*. Storyboarding makes the filmmaker's vision easier to share, saves time and can make production a whole lot simpler for every department working on the film. These things, however, cost money, and we already know that your budget is limited, so you should forgo these expensive storyboard artists. Just jot a few things down on various scraps of paper and then wing it on the day. The added beauty of not using storyboards is that your film will now have very little pace, flow or visual meaning; but as long as the audience can see something happening in front of them, and not just the inside of a lens cap, you're on to a winner.

Another advantage of winging it with your cinematographer and camera operator, Dave, is that the directions will be fresh in your mind, and will also give that rushed guerrilla-filming feel to your movie. Time may be money on a big Hollywood production, but your film has the luxury of having no planning or shooting schedule. This means you can stop the action at any time to explain to Dave what you're after in the vaguest of terms as he tries to decipher your direction. After hours of frustration, you will eventually realise that the only direction you need is, 'Make sure everybody can be seen in the shot' – and even then you will have scenes where this instruction isn't carried out. To ensure your film really is bad, you need to request that Dave include shots where all you see is the back of a person's head, where the top of an actor's face is out of shot, where two people are having a conversation spaced too far apart and – the classic – where the camera is placed at an angle, but not so much of an angle that it's clear whether the camera operator is going for a Dutch tilt or whether he or she just hasn't noticed that the tripod is collapsing.

Should you actually want to use storyboards, you need to make sure they're as personalised and confusing as possible. Put your little stick-men figures in hand-drawn boxes, ideally on the back of a script or whatever scrap paper has been left in the photocopier at your office job, and include such directions as, 'Move the camera along here for a bit' and 'Get the camera right in her face.' This is necessary because your camera operator, investor and friend whose sister you once dated, Dave, will have no idea what terms like 'POV', '2S', 'LA' and 'dolly' mean. But then, you don't really know what a dolly is either; and, let's face it, most people don't actually know what a dolly is; but it sounds good, so pop it in somewhere just to look professional.

Now you've got the idea, the script and a few bits of paper with some camera instructions on them, you're going to want to turn your attention to the actors. There are two types of actors available to those of us looking to make a low-budget travesty of a movie. The first are fresh-faced newcomers to the business who are either just out of, or still in, drama school or university; the second are low-profile porn stars who are trying to break into the legitimate film industry. The advantage of using actors fresh out of drama school is that they are keen and enthusiastic. They will look upon your no-budget movie as a thrilling adventure and be excited when you offer them only sandwiches and one can of Coke for lunch, and dinner, and breakfast. They won't complain as much when they have to stand in a freezing-cold lake for hours, and they will be happy to help with little extra jobs around the set, such as getting tea or operating the boom mic. The disadvantage, of course, is that they're not going to be so good at acting, yet. They'll still have that straight-out-of-musical-theatre smell, which means that even your most sensitive scenes will play out like a pantomime. They will also be used to working in the theatre, and will employ a number of techniques they have been taught in order to project their acting outward to a crowd instead of quietly to a camera. These include overly gesticulating, yelling all of their lines, starting each sentence with a sigh/deep breath and trying too hard to make it seem as though they are actually listening to what the other actor is saying by constantly nodding their heads and saying 'Hmm, yes, hmm' a lot.

The advantage of using ex-porn-star actors is that they will be keen to work on a movie where they can be fully clothed and their orifices can remain unstuffed for the duration of the shoot. And, unlike their previous projects, your filming isn't going to be delayed because your main cast members are in make-up having their anuses bleached. One thing that experienced porn actors have over fresh-from-drama-school actors is that they are used to being in front of a camera, so they won't freeze up, and you also won't have to spend your time yelling at them to stop looking into the lens. They will also be used to being naked on set, and the ladies will have no problem getting their boobs out, or at least be more willing to wear tight clothing and run around for no apparent reason – something that bad movie audiences are always keen on watching.

One downside to using ex-porn stars is that they probably won't be as helpful around the set. They know that they are capable of earning more than the film's entire budget in a single day, just by allowing a few old men to urinate on their face, so they will do the minimum. But the biggest downside, of course, is their film history, which – much like your internet browsing history – could have a detrimental effect on proceedings. Your film will constantly have that 'porno' vibe to it, as lines are delivered in a contrived, glazed and expressionless way. That is not to say that adult film stars haven't crossed over into the mainstream. Look at Jenna Jameson – no, not now, don't look at her now, especially if you're at work; do it at home, and use the incognito browser window. She has managed to make the leap from adult movie star to the heady mainstream heights of being the voice of a secret character in Tony Hawk's *Pro Skater 4* video and playing various other small roles as characters who are either in porn or who do things naked. You see, kids, people's perceptions of an actor *can* change.

Whichever of the two casting options you take, they are

going to prevent your film script from shining, which is exactly what we want; the more we can distract from the script, the better. Any characterisation or nuance will be eradicated, and most of your scenes will play out with the same robotic awkward tones; from romantic candlelit conversations to begging a serial killer not to stab them in the head, all of them will sound the same. But if you want to really ramp up the wooden acting, have your new actors react to something foreign to them, like an alien, or a dinosaur, or a killer zombie snow shark. This should really demonstrate their lack of range, and their eye-line will never match up to your CGI creature.

Once you've primed your actors by giving them a script a few days before filming, with no rehearsal time – because they're actors; they should already know how to act; who do they think you are, Sylvia Young? – you're finally ready to start shooting your movie, and you're going to need to inject that special bad-movie magic into the mechanics of it for the whole of the production. We already know how we're going to film it (you've bought a second-hand 8mm tape camcorder from Gumtree, you're good to go) and Dave has been primed to mount the camera on the tripod you bought at Argos and point it at the characters. Autofocus is a godsend. So now you need to think about how to light your actors.

It's a good rule of thumb when making any crappy movie to keep the audience in suspense by providing insufficient light to clearly see the set or the actors or any action that might be taking place. This makes bad-film audiences use their imaginations to create their own visuals to accompany the words they can barely hear coming from the screen. And, let's face it, their imaginations have a much bigger budget than you do, so they can only make your movie better. For example, if you want to create a sense of tension during a scene in a horror movie, you want to keep the audience guessing. So it's encouraging to hear them saying things like, 'Oh no, he's gone into the house, I think. Is that the living-room? It must be. I'm sure I can make out a sofa. Or that might be a bed. That could be a bedroom. Hang on, where did the killer go? Is that him there in the corner? That might be a lamp. Oh no, he's found her, I think, unless that's a blanket box, or a dog. That could be a dog. Why would they have a dog? He's got his knife out and he's cutting her throat. Oh, no he isn't, he's making a sandwich. False alarm. That's not the killer, that's the babysitter.'

If you're going to be filming a night-time scene, remember that the bigger and better productions will use key lighting to make it look like night-time, so that the actors can still be seen by the audience. For a bad movie, you have a number of choices. You can actually film at night, creating a dancing tapestry of silhouettes against a navy background, or you can use the cinematic trick of shooting 'day-for-night'. Day-for-night is a technique that was used mostly in made-for-TV films in the '70s and '80s. It involves scenes being filmed in the day but with a coloured filter used to make it seem darker. I would recommend your bad movie use this technique, as long as you remember not to buy an actual filter but just nip down to Tesco for some blue-coloured cellophane that you can stick over the camera lens with sticky tape. Also, be sure to film your day-for-night scenes at noon on the sunniest day of the year. That way, you will not only be able to see the actors and the sets clearly through the filter, but the bright sun will cast obvious shadows, giving your film that eerie and otherworldly 'brightest moon ever' feel to it. Also, because of the quality of your actors, they will be squinting during their scenes. This may look strange, but at least they will actually be reacting to something, which will give your bad movie the acting boost it so desperately needs.

If things are just too dark, then borrow or buy a builder's or workman's light to shine on the action. But only the one. Shadowless three-key lighting is fine for those who want the audience to get lost in the naturalism of a scene, but your actors are the most important part of your film, so be sure to shine that strong light directly onto their faces. If there are two actors in a scene that contains a shot of them standing or sitting together, then you are going to have to pick a favourite and light that one. Plus, again, shadows will give your film a noir feel and help promote it as an independent art film. The more shadows, the more laurel leaves you can put on your DVD cover. The exception to this rule is that any CGI creatures you are using should, inexplicably, have no shadows at all.

Now that *most* of your actors can be seen, it's time to focus on the sound. Your typical big-budget Hollywood mainstream movie will have sound bods all over the place – boom mic operators, sound recordists, engineers etc – but you will want to opt either for having a film student hold a karaoke microphone strapped to a broom handle, or for simply using the microphone that's on the front of your Gumtree-bought camcorder. Using the microphone that's attached to the camera has the added bonus of making any dialogue spoken in a long-shot almost inaudible. This will then switch to painfully loud when you cut to a close-up.

It is very important when making a bad movie to ensure that sounds such as footsteps, glasses being placed on tables, and chairs creaking are much louder than the actors' voices. Whereas most filmmakers strive to capture 'clean sound' (where, as previously discussed, only the actors' voices are recorded, all the other sounds being dubbed on later by the foley artist) you are looking for 'dirty sound'. Try to get as much car noise, plane sounds and windy weather onto your film as possible, so that the audience will have to work that much harder to hear what the actors are saying. They'll already be trying to see what's going on with the one who has his back to them; having a few mumbled lines delivered some way off from the microphone is only going to enhance their experience. If you can find any copyright-free music to use, use it. Don't bother checking if it's suitable for the scene; you can call it an 'artistic choice'. Nobody else will have used Herb Alpert's 'Spanish Flea' to underscore a multiple murder.

There might be times when you have to use ADR – which means automated dialogue replacement or, in layman's terms, having the actors talk over their original lines because they can't be heard. This should be used only if the sound levels are wrong, the actors' lines are totally lost, the background noises are too loud or the microphone has failed to record any sound at all. This means that you should need to do ADR for most of your movie. Your set-up should include a laptop on which to show the scene, your karaoke mic freed from its broomstick and balanced on a tower of books, and a nervous or confused actor whose timing is so bad that he or she isn't even able to sync up a previously-spoken line. Sometimes an actor will be so bad or have an accent so strong that it ruins even your terrible movie. If this happens, then you can get another actor in to sync over the lines. But remember to get an actor who is going to be just as bad as the previous one, if not slightly worse. If you handle it correctly, the ADR will give the audience the added bonus of some actors sounding louder than others, and some of them speaking slightly out of sync with their lip movements.

If you are planning to include a creature in your movie – a shark, a giant spider, a space monkey etc – then sound is going to be extra-important. Not only will you need to recreate the sounds of its environment – the ocean, a spindly web, some kind of space jungle – but you are also going to have to assign it a voice. In nature, sharks don't roar and spiders don't scream, and I would assume that if nobody can hear you scream in space, they certainly can't hear your space monkey's chattering threats. But this shouldn't deter you from adding these sounds to give your movie another layer of improbability. If the makers of *Shark Attack 3* and *Jaws The Revenge* can have their shark roar like a lion as it leaps out of the water, then there is no reason why you can't make your space earwig screech like that fat kid who set his balls on fire on that YouTube video.

Once all the film is in the can, or on a stack of 8mm tapes, it's time to stick the movie together. There is a multitude of professional-standard editing software available, such as Adobe Premier Pro, Sony Vegas Pro and Final Cut Pro, but you're not a pro, so stick with what you're comfortable with and, most importantly, what's free. This means that your bad movie will be skilfully put together by yourself on your home computer using Windows Movie Maker. Even though you usually use your computer only for Facebook and Google, needs must, the film must be completed. The advantage of editing your film yourself is that you know what you're looking for when it comes to choosing the right takes in the right scenes. Plus, you're a lot cheaper than a professional editor, who will want actual money in exchange for his or her skills. Good editing ensures a seamless journey through a movie, a swift and slick transition from one scene to the next, so flawless that the audience believe they are watching one long continuous shot. What you need to achieve is a jerky, rhythm-less hour and thirty minutes of long pauses, obvious cuts and clock-wipe transitions. Ideally what you want to be doing is making the film seem as awkward as possible, wringing all of the tension out by not cutting to the action fast enough, and by having the quick-paced fight sequences draw themselves out to the point where it seems the protagonists are fighting underwater. If editing is all about rhythm, you will need to posses the timing skills of a drunk dancing uncle at a wedding.

Using a variety of shots to keep the attention of the audience is a must, but if you can find a pattern or a rhythm to cutting between them, then it's going to make your job a lot easier. I would wholeheartedly suggest that all scenes follow this pattern: long-shot, mid-shot, two-shot, head-shot, close-up (doesn't matter if it's a close-up of the actor talking, the other actor trying to make out that he or she is listening or a random close up of a cup of coffee, just as long as you get one in there), mid-shot, long-shot and repeat. This way, the audience gets to relax and enjoy the comfort of the predictably of shots, so that they can go back to trying to figure out the story, the acting, the setting and what the actors are actually saying. During a sex-having scene, you can save time and embarrassment for your actors – apart from your ex-porno actors, of course – by just looping the same shots over and over again. If your actors have their abs and boobs out, nobody is going to notice that you've shown the same shot of her bouncing up and down on his belly button four times, or him rubbing her boobs in the same place for three minutes.

As well as the blindingly obvious mistakes, there are some subtleties that you can bring to your editing that can just set your film off kilter. At the end of a scene, leave just enough space between the last line and the cut to the next scene; make it just long enough that the audience anticipate a line of dialogue from another actor, or a bit of action, and then snap it to black and fade up somewhere else. You can also go the other way, and have the actors in the new scene start talking before the fade up from black has fully transitioned. This tells your audience that the dialogue is so important that the director just couldn't wait for the scene actually to start before letting them hear it. The one thing that phone-in reality talent shows have taught us is that people really love to be kept waiting to find out information. Take a leaf out of their book and build tension by leaving really, really long gaps between important lines of dialogue. Cut away to a tree or a brook or a lovely sunset; your audience will thank you for making them wait so long to be disappointed.

Your bad movie has now been filmed, edited and scored with a copyright-free CD or your own recording of various chords on a Bontempi organ. This means that you are finally ready to unleash it on the world. Even though you don't possess the same marketing and graphics skills as your average Hollywood mainstream studio or production company, you do have a basic graphics package, a DVD burner on your laptop and, by now, a relentless confidence in yourself and your film. You've printed out your DVD covers, which are in stylish black and white (which is cheaper to print) and sports a picture of your main protagonists in tight-fitting clothing, standing by a generic building. You've bought your DVD boxes from eBay and a hundred padded envelopes and you're ready to go.

You can submit your terrible film to a variety of film festivals, but most of them charge a fee, which you will never see again, and they also tend to fill up their programmes with good movies – which is a little short-sighted if you ask me; there should be *some* variation in quality. You don't need these festivals anyway; they're run by a bunch of privileged, toffee-nosed, la-di-da film students, who will sip their Coffeccinos and look down on your production because it's an alien space romantic comedy set in the future and not a whimsical movie about domestic violence or racism. The best course of action you can take is to e-mail video links of your movie and post out hard copies to any and every company on IMDB Pro that has a distribution credit. It doesn't matter if they specialise in nature documentaries or religious movies, send it to them all. Be sure to include a note that explains the plot of the movie and how ground-breaking it is, and don't forget to add how they will be sure to make millions off of it, especially if they agree to make the sequel, and that they will be kicking themselves repeatedly if they miss this golden opportunity and you have to go with another company.

If any of these companies are kind enough to contact you with a polite notice thanking you for sending them the movie but stating that it isn't something they are looking to distribute at the moment, you should immediately take it personally and compose a snarky response. This should be needlessly aggressive in tone. Be sure you insist that they explain in detail every single reason for their rejection of the movie and justify why they are not going to distribute it. Be sure also to end the reply with an unconvincing line about how you don't really care about their opinion, and how you're going to make it big without them, whatever.

The best course of action is to hire a small cinema in the West End of London and hold your own première. Invite as many of the cast as you can, as well as Dave, along with any and every film blogger, reviewer and national newspaper, with the promise of free drinks and snacks that you ultimately won't be able to afford or deliver. Once the film has been shown, assert your confidence even more by demanding that there be a Q&A session with the director once the credits have rolled. You need to spend the next half an hour cajoling people into asking insipid and general questions such as, 'Where do you get your ideas from?', and then spend twenty minutes answering them while referencing your 'body of work'. During the Q&A session, be sure to plant somebody in the audience who will say, 'This isn't so much a question as an observation.' Every

Q&A session needs at least two of those to annoy the audience.

Once the première is over and none of your invited media guests have shown up or written about your movie, it's time to take it to the people. The internet. Here your movie isn't restricted by age constraints, venue fees, geographical limitations or filters. Here it can exist on the most level of playing fields, where upwards of two billion people could potentially view it. But remember that, on the internet, the most interesting and poignant of movies are no match for a video of a tiny cat falling off a table into a shoe. If there comes a point, and this is rare, where you encounter a comment under your movie that isn't as positive as you might have hoped, then you should engage with that person, enter into a discussion on why he or she thinks your film is 'gay' or 'worse than Hitler' or why they think you are a 'talentless cock-fucking ball-face'. With a little conversation you could probably change their minds. After all, people on the internet are inherently reasonable, and you could gain a lot of valuable feedback for your next movie.

Put links on as many forums, websites and other videos' comment sections as possible. Really get the word out there, and then spend the next few months alone, in your underwear, putting the name of your movie into various search engines every hour until you finally find it in a Buzz feed list of '100 worst films ever made'. Now it is time to do your victory dance, because now you know that you have made it.

So there you have it in a nutshell; how to make the best possible cinematic travesty you can. If you stick to this guide, you will find making bad movies is both addictive and enjoyable. All you have to remember is that this is *your* vanity project, and this is going to be *your* ticket to showing everybody that can write and shoot a feature film with no training and no past experience, and that, no, you're not delusional or an idiot and, actually, you are going to prove to your parents that you were right not to go to university or take that job in the post office that your mum's friend Eileen got you an interview for. Now you can tell people you're a *bona fide* filmmaker; but not any old filmmaker, one of the worst. You can honestly tell people who say they have never heard of you or your work that there is a real buzz around it. Just never tell them that the buzz is actually coming from all the flies circling your turd of a movie.

A Word from My Friends

When writing this book, I asked many friends in the bad-movie community as well as those who work in the industry to give me an insight into their favourite movies, scenes and characters. I got many great and funny responses but just wasn't able to use them all in the main text. So I've dedicated this part of the book to all of those who helped me, and I thought it would be nice to include a few of their answers to my questions.

Elliott Kalan

I'm partial to bad science fiction movies, because the deck is stacked against the filmmakers right from the top. They need to create convincing special effects, and usually they can't do that. It also opens the door for moments you won't find in other genres. In the movie *R.O.T.O.R.* (1987), the hero works at a science lab staffed by a robot janitor who is bumbling and forgetful. It makes no sense why a robot would be programmed to be basically a stoner flake. It almost feels like they wrote the part of 'goofy janitor' and then a robot showed up at the audition, aced the part, and was hired. Bad comedies are almost never fun to sit through. They're just death. To see someone fail at making an exciting or inspiring scene is funny, to see someone fail at being funny is infuriating.

Adam Spiegelman

The Room just caught lightning in a bottle. There's no denying that it has all the elements of a great bad film. Bad shots, bad acting, bad script and an actor replaced in the middle of the film. In LA, it started with midnight screenings. I noticed a lot of film students showing up. There's something cathartic about watching everything that could go wrong, go wrong. All your biggest fears are on the screen. One screening, a college kid behind me said he'd never seen the movie before and wasn't sure what to expect. Halfway through the film, he tapped me on the shoulder and screamed, 'I will never be the same again!'

Rod Woodhouse

A 'good' bad movie is either one that is enjoyable because of its crapness or one that is enjoyable despite its crapness. The former is more likely to be well aware that it is a bad movie and so gives the opportunity to poke fun at itself and let the audience know the filmmakers share the enjoyment of the badness. It can also take itself seriously, but invites the audience to make fun of it as it goes along and enjoy the process of deconstructing the movie.

Claire Vaughan

The Bad Film Club introduced me to the joy of *I Know Who Killed Me* (2007). A Lindsay Lohan vehicle made at the very point she started to take herself very seriously and started to take acting less so. It helps that the director either didn't understand the story or the producers edited the film to the extent that the plot makes no sense and the twist feels like an afterthought. Everything about it is terrible, but I don't think anyone quite realised how bad it was going to be till it was finished.

Tristan Jones

'Bad' bad films are slow, tiresome, lethargic and predictable. They may have an irritating main character who sits in the limelight unnecessarily (such as the horrendous little girl played by Dakota Fanning in the 2005 *War of the Worlds*). A 'bad' bad film has a plot that doesn't really go anywhere

(*Skew* (2011)), or production values so low that schoolchildren could do better. The worst bad films are the sorts that are clearly nothing more than a paean to the vanity of those who put the film together.

Ti Singh

There is something fundamentally fascinating about a bad film. Whether it is the bargain-basement special effects or the fact they clearly didn't care about lighting, continuity or even a script. That is why they are so infinitely entertaining. You just wonder how the hell this got made and if this is really what the filmmakers wanted to make. That's what bad movies often are – someone's dream that, despite their earnestness, failed to translate to screen in the way they hoped (or in some cases *exactly* in the way they hoped!)

Paul Maskell

I find it hard to forgive bad big studio pictures. With all of the resources thrown at them, not to produce something entertaining seems a sin. Pretty much summed up by all of M Night Shyamalan's post *Unbreakable* (2000) output.

Kelly Steel

The way in which Tommy Wiseau can't even laugh convincingly (or on cue). The way in which the director/writer/producer/star is such a massive egomaniac he managed to make an absolute turd of a film and convince the world that not only should you see it at least once, you should encourage other people to see it too and pay through the nose for the privilege. It's like Soylent Green; highly addictive, but you know that there's something in there that isn't quite right.

About the Author

Dr Nicko Vaughan started out as a stand-up comedian back in 1996 when, at the age of 21, and after only two gigs, she performed in the final of the 'open mic' competition *The Stand Up Show*, which was broadcast on BBC One. It was also around this time that she started writing for the comedy magazines *Deadpan* and *Comedy Review* and became a contributor to the book *Dates from Hell*.

After a stint writing radio sketches and performing more stand-up comedy, she turned her back on the comedy world to pursue a career in the film industry. Here she became a script supervisor on a variety of independent films, short movies, television adverts and music videos, which would stand her in good stead for her passion-turned-career later in life.

In 2004, she was once more drawn to comedy, and wrote the stage show *Songs We Think We Know*, which she performed with her comedy partner Joe Timmins at the 2004 Melbourne International Comedy Festival. After receiving critical acclaim for that show, she returned in 2005 with another, *Appetite for Distraction*, before writing a third, *Nicko& Joe Sell Out*, which she performed at the 2005 Edinburgh Fringe Festival.

Her script *Death Plays Black*, a serialised disaster film for the radio, was shortlisted for the BBC Witty and Twisted Award, and she was commissioned to write and perform a promo ident for the Summer of British Film season on BBC Two, and for pilots on various projects for Talkback Thames. She also had a stint reviewing DVD releases and presenting *The Comedy Zone* on BBC 7/BBC Radio 4 Extra, as well as reviewing films in her column for *New Empress* magazine.

In 2006 she set up the interactive Bad Film Club from an idea she and Joe had kicked around while at the Edinburgh Fringe the previous year, and she has been writing and producing the show (including performances at Cardiff Chapter Arts Centre and the Barbican Centre in London) and touring it internationally ever since. In 2008 she also organised the first Bad Film Club Film Festival at the Barbican, where actress Jenny McShane, star of *Shark Attack 3*, accepted the award for best bad movie of all time. Bad films continue to be her passion, and she now uses them as a cautionary example in her lectures on screenwriting at the University of Swansea, where she is part of the Creative Writing Department.

55053306R00121

Made in the USA
Charleston, SC
17 April 2016